God GLASSES

To Paul

Don Mounts

ANN MONSTER

GOD GLASSES

Copyright © 2017 Ann Monster.

All rights reserved. No part of this book may be used or reproduced by any means, graphic, electronic, or mechanical, including photocopying, recording, taping or by any information storage retrieval system without the written permission of the author except in the case of brief quotations embodied in critical articles and reviews.

Cover art by Emma Delazzari.

iUniverse books may be ordered through booksellers or by contacting:

iUniverse
1663 Liberty Drive
Bloomington, IN 47403
www.iuniverse.com
1-800-Authors (1-800-288-4677)

Because of the dynamic nature of the Internet, any web addresses or links contained in this book may have changed since publication and may no longer be valid. The views expressed in this work are solely those of the author and do not necessarily reflect the views of the publisher, and the publisher hereby disclaims any responsibility for them.

Any people depicted in stock imagery provided by Thinkstock are models, and such images are being used for illustrative purposes only.
Certain stock imagery © Thinkstock.

ISBN: 978-1-5320-1774-2 (sc)
ISBN: 978-1-5320-1775-9 (e)

Library of Congress Control Number: 2017903203

Print information available on the last page.

iUniverse rev. date: 03/29/2017

Also by Ann Monster
I Love You—Letters from a Loving Friend
I Hear You
You and I Am

To you, the reader, regardless of who you are, what you have or have not done, how rich or poor you are, how educated or uneducated you are, how young or old you are, or whether you are male or female, your God will meet you face-to-face exactly where you are on your path the moment you invite Him to join you. No judgments made!

In loving memory of my husband, Bert

CONTENTS

Introduction xi
A Note from the Scribe xiii
Obedience versus Intimate Friendship 1
How Does God Want Us to See Him? 3
Do I Take the Lead in My Movie, or Am I Just an Extra? 9
Allowing Spirit to Interpret Scripture 12
Free Choice ... Really? 15
What Sort of an Attitude Do I Bring to the Table? 19
How to Hear God 22
Living in Fear or Living in Love 25
Does Satan Exist? 28
Marital Difficulties 30
What Is Needed for a Lasting Marriage 34
Unconditional Love 37
Treating Others as You Would Like Them to Treat You 40
9/11 44
Reaction versus Proaction 47
A Paradigm Shift 50
Less Judgment—More Compassion 55
Expectations 57
Many Paths to Finding Relationship with Your God 62
Vulnerability 65

Dare to Make a Difference	68
Sexuality	70
Homosexuality	76
Dealing with Anxiety	79
You Have My Permission to Ask Questions	84
The Unfolding of Truth	87
Dare to Risk Finding Truth	91
Momentary Thoughts and Feedback	96
Using God	98
Using God (Continued)	101
Knowing and Appreciating Oneself	103
Regarding the Death of a Loved One	107
A Message on Christmas Eve	110
A New Year's Message	113
Same-Sex Marriages	116
A Crime or an Accident Waiting to Happen	119
Fear Keeps You and I Apart	122
Now or in God's Time!	125
Learning to Accept Responsibility	128
The Mechanics of Healing a Faltering Marriage	131
When Praying for Others	134
Love Heals	136
HIV/AIDS	139
Eradicating Poverty	141
Rethinking Sexuality	145
A Mature and Responsible Approach to Sexuality	149
Reincarnation: Questions and Answers	154
A Definitive Response	160
The Evolution of Spirituality	163
A Healing Update	168
Another Healing Update	172
Learning How to Appreciate Ourselves	174

More Healing Documentations 177
The Power of Positive Thinking 182
The Importance of Truly Knowing Ourselves 185
All in God's Timing 189
Doing It Jesus' Way 193
Chaos—Where Do We Begin? 196
Living within Time 199
Bon Voyage! 202

INTRODUCTION

By the age of thirty-five, fear and anxiety enslaved me. Though I had graduated as a registered nurse a few years prior, I was by then a full-time mother of two. One particularly stressful night, I crawled onto the bed with tightly clenched teeth and silently yelled, "God, I would just like to relax for a minute!"

Instantly all anxiety disappeared! Wondering what on earth had happened, I was looking around the darkened bedroom when a vision of Christ, holding a child by the hand, appeared. I sensed I had heard, "Trust me!" Incredible peace filled me, and I sank into a deep sleep.

When I awakened the next morning, I felt transformed, and confirmation came when my young daughter looked at me and said, "Mommy, you're different!"

Deeply affected, I began to search out this Healer. A thought crossed my mind one day after morning meditation. If Christ walked the face of the earth today, I wonder what He would say.

Later, while preparing to write in my journal, I was surprised to find myself penning what seemed like dictation and the initial letter of what would eventually become my first book, *I Love You—Letters from a Loving Friend*, flowed onto the page.

This volume of communications, *God Glasses*, endeavors to explain life and many of its aspects from the perspective of the Creator who talks to all His beloved children, regardless of race, creed, age, gender, position, possessions, goodness, or brokenness. As He has communicated time and time again, *"I love you all equally, and I will meet you exactly where you are on your path the minute you ask me to join you. Always remember, if something is happening, then I have allowed it. If I have allowed it, therefore it has purpose. So know there is a jewel to be found if you persist."*

I hope the responses and clarifications to some of my more recent queries and experiences will encourage you, the reader, to search out personal dialogue and intimate friendship with your Creator God.

A NOTE FROM THE SCRIBE

I have written this volume of communication to help us realize that we are all unique in God's eyes. We have been given free choice, and He will work closely with us as we make those decisions, acknowledging us for wise ones and encouraging us to choose again when a choice is/was not the best. He offers us alternative ways of looking at our life's experiences.

The longer I walk this spiritual journey, the more I come to realize that, even though most of us are all believing in God (Jehovah, Allah, the Trinity, Buddha, or Source), there are major differences in basic tenets and an infinite number of divergent minutia that seem to keep us from unity and Oneness.

Even in small groups, there can be disagreement that can cause people to take sides. How can we ever hope to find unity in this world when even a handful of persons have difficulty finding common ground around such issues as fasting or the correct degree of reverence?

God, might You have some insight for us?

☙

I most assuredly do!

OBEDIENCE VERSUS INTIMATE FRIENDSHIP

I've been reading Phillip Yancey's book, *Reaching for the Invisible God*. It amazes me that, even after twenty-plus years of a definite faith journey, I can still find myself at times doubting my credibility as a person in relationship with her God. I can be feeling quite certain that I am on the right track when someone suddenly says something or I read another thing that appears to negate what seems to be emerging as truth.

On a recent retreat, I apparently offended a few people in our group when they interpreted something I said as, "It was not necessary to be in awe of God." Am I getting too casual with You, Lord?

☙

GG I wish to respond here, for this is an area of contention for many of you. A healthy respect for something that is powerful is always a good idea. A skilled electrician is always respectful of the nature of the power he works with, but that does not stop him from doing his work or cause him to work in fear. A knowledgeable wild animal handler knows his subject well enough to allow him to do his job skillfully and without fear, yet he is always conscious of his subject's potential.

Ann Monster

Human beings who truly know God are always respectful and in awe of Me, but that never prevents them from experiencing an intimate friendship with Me. Awe and respect that keeps a soul from experiencing My love, My compassion, or My acceptance is not true awe and respect but an immature level of belief.

Just like the novice electrician, a certain degree of uncertainty should be present to begin with, but a relationship with Me should eventually lead you beyond fear and feelings of unworthiness. An authentic relationship with Me does not diminish your awe and respect for Me, but it does produce a knowing beyond a shadow of a doubt that I am here for you. That happens automatically when you have learned that you can come to Me with any thought, concern, or feeling, knowing I will listen quietly, discuss calmly, instruct gently, love always, and, in the end, give you My permission to make your own decision based on what we have just discussed.

When you have relationship like this with Me, you never lose that natural awe and respect, which eventually grows into love for Me. And love changes everything. (Yes, I most certainly gave ALW[1] the inspiration for that one!) I note your obedience, and I acknowledge your respect, but I treasure your love for Me.

I am love, AKA God O-O

---

[1] Andrew Lloyd Webber

HOW DOES GOD WANT US TO SEE HIM?

*D*oubt, uncertainty, fear, and even indifference, these emotions seem to surface frequently if you get into any sort of in-depth conversation with people these days.

The person whose marriage has become quite painful, the employee who hates his job but sees no alternative for several reasons, or the adult son or daughter who watches powerlessly as a beloved parent slowly disappears behind the stealth of Alzheimer's all pray for answers, healing, direction, or resolution, sometimes for years, with no obvious response from You.

What would be an appropriate response, Lord, when anger and frustration erupt at the mention of prayer, patience, or "in God's time"? What do You suggest when we've gotten just too worn out from the personal journey?

☙

GG I hear you, and I most certainly wish to respond to these kinds of situations. Surprisingly I do understand the frustration and eventual anger that can blind a person to the reality of what is truly transpiring at any given moment or in any set of circumstances. You, My scribe, feel frustration as you write this, for you are recalling real examples of the frustrations that certain people whom you know are experiencing at this time. You are unable to figure out how to fix it for them, that is, to ease their anguish. You see no apparent solutions.

As you well know, I am not in the habit of revealing outcomes or futures because the actual playing out of these journeys is important for the souls involved. What we can do here for clarification is dissect a story or two that has already served the purpose for which it was allowed. Remember, if something is occurring, then I have allowed it. And if I have allowed it, then it has purpose.

Take, for instance, the story of Jesus, My Son and your brother. Here was a human being, in every way like any one of you. He lived what you would call a good and holy life and was crucified for it in the end. (For those of you who need to hear My name mentioned with reverence, please bear with us here.) This is clarification for the angry and broken. If you have been graced enough to have come out of your trials with your faith intact, say "thank You" and give the others here a chance to try to understand what might have been missed in their journey of spiritual formation.

I said that Jesus was like any one of you. He had built into Him all the natural needs and desires that are built into you. What He did not have was the brokenness or baggage that most of you eventually find yourselves carrying around in life. You may not have been given choices as to what baggage was handed to you, but you most certainly do have choices as to how you respond to those challenges. You can allow them to cripple you, weighing you down with anger and self-pity, or you can take note of your reactions to them, looking for the less obvious and more proactive response that frees you of the burden, rewarding you with increasing wisdom and/ or smarts.

Remember the term, "God made man." Think of Me as creating a soul, a human being, and then squeezing Myself into that form. (And believe Me, it was a tight squeeze.) All the human traits were there, but what was also there was the mind of God. This can best be expressed as meeting each situation in life by asking, "What can I do to help bring about the best or optimum resulting outcome?" In simpler terms, "What do I have to do to make the best of this situation?" Put on your God glasses. Comprehend with My wisdom.

So through the existence of Jesus, I was able to experience what it is like to be human; therefore I can relate to what any one of you might be going through at any moment in time. The limited account of Jesus' life in the New Testament gives you evidence that, if you are willing, it is humanly possible to go through one's life experiencing the best possible outcome for all.

Yes, Jesus (I in human form) died on a cross. I allowed Myself to be crucified just so you would all come to realize that human death is not the end of life to be feared and dreaded but merely a reunion with Me, the Creator of all things. You are all made in the image and likeness of Me. You all have built into you what Jesus had built into Him. You need only recognize it and choose to use it. Everyone has the ability to see with My eyes. You only need to want to.

You will find that you cease to scream at Me or plead with Me to change this or take that away. You will discover a quiet inside that merely requests that I teach you how to cope so the best can come of this situation.

I know what it is like to feel alone, abandoned, terrified, and hurt emotionally and physically and to face inevitable human death. I am not having this written to make you believe in Me or to fill churches. I am not having this written because I expect obedience and respect. I am having this written down so you might realize that I do hear you. I am listening. I do care, and every situation has the potential of a positive outcome!

You see, I know all the reasons why you are at this point where you scoff and say, "Yah, right!" I know all the hurts, abuses, disappointments, failures, and self-doubt that you carry with you every day. I accept and love you just as much as I accept and love that person whom you would give anything to be like. Imagine!

Imagine being accepted and loved in exactly the form you are in right now. Imagine being accepted and loved regardless of your looks, intelligence, success, or failure, in spite of the things you have or have not done. Imagine being loved even though you are convinced that no one would love you if they knew that you had—!

Mankind, when not wearing God glasses, has an infinite capacity for judgment, condemnation, and punishment. I, on the other hand, have an infinite capacity to observe, instruct, and love.

You now have a choice to make. You can choose to see Me as all loving, or you can decide to believe in a whimsical God who has good and bad days, says one thing but means another, and asserts that you have free choice but then punishes you if you appear to have chosen wrongly. You can believe that I am more interested in you for going to church on Sunday and saying a certain number of prayers. A God like that arises out of ancient folklore.

I have given you the ability to think, analyze, and make decisions. Use that gift at this time, and decide to discover for yourself the one true God. In spite of what some people actually believe, I do not doom souls to eternal damnation. Why not give the idea of an all-loving God a chance—one who created you for eternal life and life in abundance here on earth—now?

Scribe, We said earlier that We'd dissect a couple stories to make a point of how negative or even tragic circumstances will always have potentially positive outcomes. The story you are best equipped to dissect is your own. Even though it continues to evolve, certainly aspects of the past have already been illuminated as conveyances to an optimum outcome.

The absence of love and all that love nourishes in an infant, child, and teen; the inability to love and accept yourself due to others' myopic view of what was important; and the experience of life continuously in anxiety, interrupted only by periodic panic attacks, have been a few of the more negative aspects of your journey, yet you are now the first to express appreciation for them.

How could you ever have appreciated with such intensity the awareness and feeling of My love for you if it had not been for that absence of any love from those around you? How can one know hot if one has never experienced cold? Without contrasts, man is unable to experience awareness. How could you ever have felt the incredible awe of knowing that I loved you just as you were if others' rejection of how you looked had not convinced you that you were unlovable? How could you ever have been convinced beyond a shadow of a doubt that I existed if there had not been something of which I could relieve you in an instant?

For years, you experienced constant anxiety, and in one brief moment, it was gone and has not returned. If it had not been for these circumstances, you would not have become who you are, and you would not be writing any of this.

You have asked Me, "Why me, Lord?" You have asked that with both awe and/or frustration.

I have responded with, "Why not you?" Why would you not have to experience trials and adversity when life and all it encompasses has inherent trials and adversity? If I needed someone to do a specific task, requiring a certain personality to blend with a unique set of learning experiences, why would I not pick you? I needed someone, and you met all the qualifications. And if your journey does have some inherent gifts that go with this package, might I suggest that you enjoy them! This is basically common sense.

One final word on this subject to anyone who might read this material, think! Think about what has been said here. Ponder it. Does it make sense? Does it speak to your heart? If it does not, then let it go and get on with life as you know it. You may already be light-years beyond this kind of thinking, or life, as you are experiencing it, is serving you well, thank you very much.

If it does speak to your heart and a part of you wants to go there, then come, keep the brain focused on finding the one true God, and know that, if you sincerely desire to find Me, I will not allow you to get irretrievably lost down some momentary detour in the road. Trust Me! This directive was the first that this scribe ever heard from Me, and she's still learning how many years later.

God O-O

DO I TAKE THE LEAD IN MY MOVIE, OR AM I JUST AN EXTRA?

*D*ear God, am I right in thinking that You are nudging me to pick up this pen?

☙

GG Yes, My scribe, I would like us to reflect on this morning. You started out the day by allowing what was on your agenda to affect your mood. You were due back at the surgeon's office to get the results of the cone biopsy that had been done a month prior. Part of you felt reasonably confident that the results would be favorable because you probably would have been called back sooner if further surgery or treatment were deemed necessary. Another part of you was entertaining worry thoughts, what ifs.

What if I (God) could use your experience of being diagnosed with cancer and the inherent surgery and chemo or radiation therapy to help those people who are receiving such a diagnosis? Annie, you often amaze Me where you go with that imagination of yours, but I will give you credit. You are beginning to see with My glasses. You are beginning to see yourself as having a choice as to what sort of a role you might play against the backdrop of your day-to-day life circumstances.

By the time you were driving to the medical building, you had pretty much put away the worry thoughts and chosen to accept whatever role I may be asking you to play, be it one demanding courage and dignity or mere relief and gratitude. As you got out of the car, you had assumed the role of leading lady, and you made eye contact (where you could) with passersby and smiled. You were at peace in the waiting room and quite composed with the doctor even during the examination.

The clean bill of health that you received did not hit you like a wave of relief, as you would have expected. Even as you got off the elevator, you made a point of speaking to someone you had not seen in years. She had not noticed you, and as you learned while talking with her, she was preoccupied and worried regarding the appointment that she was about to keep.

Her circumstances were dictating to her how she was feeling and where her focus was. She was unaware that she had a choice as to how she addressed these circumstances, and she was allowing the fear of the unknown to dictate those feelings.

As you stood chatting together, a little elderly woman, whose breathing seemed labored, appeared. She was having difficulty seeing which elevator button to push. When you asked if she would like some help, she queried which floor her doctor was on, and between you and your friend, you provided her with the information she needed from the directory on the wall.

As the elevator door opened, your friend immediately stepped on with her, looked you in the eye with a smile, and assured you that she would make sure that this distressed old soul got to her destination. How readily your friend stepped onto the elevator in spite of the fact that, in doing so, it would take her another step closer to the circumstances that she had convinced herself were to be dreaded. Suddenly she was directing the moment rather than allowing the moment to direct her. She had ceased to play an involuntary role in a play not of her choosing and had taken over the lead.

You all have the choice of allowing life to force you to play a role that you do not wish to take on, or you can choose to take the lead in the circumstances in which you find yourself at any given moment. You can allow others to define how your role is to be portrayed, or you may write your own script with all its inherent importance and impact. There are always options.

"How well would I have continued to play the lead if the doctor had told me that there was a problem", *you are thinking*. What about the people who read this and are facing an actual serious diagnosis? How helpful is this story to them?

Ann, everyone, including you, has faced uncertain situations, bad news, and disappointments in the past, and they will in the future. The point we are making here is that everyone has the choice as to how he or she chooses to handle his or her role in these circumstances. There is no written script, but one directive is recommended in any situation. Ask Me for advice as to how best to respond to any given situation.

As one begins to do this, you may not always be completely pleased with your performance, but as time passes and you get to know Me better, your ability to hear My responses and to follow My cues will improve dramatically. Instead of dreading each scene of every act, you will be amazed by your own performance and how truly interesting the story line really is. You will live in the present, be interested in the moment, and not be just white-knuckling it to the finale.

I'm here whenever you need Me. I'll show you how to use God glasses.

God O-O

ALLOWING SPIRIT TO
INTERPRET SCRIPTURE

Yesterday I was thumbing through a book that a friend had given us, *Amazing Grace* by Kathleen Norris. Each chapter addresses a different topic, and one in particular caught my eye. It was entitled "Lectio Divina." Normally I would have bypassed this as something I am too unschooled to comprehend, but for some reason, I felt drawn to continue. She defines *lectio divina* as holy reading, and as I read on, I got the sense that it meant allowing scripture to speak to one personally in one's own set of circumstances.

As this manuscript is developing format, it seemed it might be worthwhile to start to read the New Testament, and if a particular passage spoke specifically to me, should it be included in this book followed by commentary as seen through Your eyes? After just happening across this chapter on *lectio divina*, I feel convinced I should at least try it out.

Lord, do You wish to comment on this idea?

Ann, I was beginning to wonder just how many nudges I would have to come up with before you actually followed through. Congratulations! Only two! Let's give it a try.

☙

Papa, I started with Matthew, and I was going to skip Jesus' genealogy, but You said to read it. I got stuck on the realization that this is, in actuality, Joseph's lineage, but if You are the Father of Jesus and not Joseph, then this is not Jesus' genealogy. A genealogy of Mary might be more fitting. The pen is Yours, Papa/Spirit.

☙

GG Annie, you are absolutely right. Joseph's lineage does not justify Jesus as a descendant of a long line of famous Jewish patriarchs. Mary's lineage does justify him as a Jew, but of course, the writers of this book felt obligated to legitimize Jesus, and only paternal genealogy was considered valid. The wisdom and faith of people today is able to overlook ancient (and not so ancient) ignorance and prejudice. What Mary truly did was legitimize Jesus' humanity.

Except for My divine involvement, Jesus was born of a woman, just as every other human being has been born since humans have walked the face of this world. Today it can be understood that it is not so important that Jesus was a Jew, but He was the personification of God whose life, death, and resurrection confirmed a new Covenant of love, forgiveness, and eternal salvation for all of mankind. His humanity makes Me approachable. As Jesus was quoted as saying, "If you know Me, you know the Father."

I wish to be loved. Any one of you who has children that you truly love does not look for praise and adoration from them. You look for simply love. This is a love based in deep trust, admiration, and understanding of whom you are. Consider what is being said here, and govern yourself accordingly. Search Me out through My Son to develop an intimate relationship with Us. You will find the kingdom right here on earth for yourself and, in doing so, help it to become a reality for others. We await you.

God O-O

FREE CHOICE ... REALLY?

*J*esus, this morning You seem so real! Bruce Clinton's book, *Rabbi Jesus*, refers to You as probably seen as a *mamzer*.[2] There is so little that we truly know about You and what those thirty-three years really were like. They must have been difficult years. Yet as I wonder why Scripture leaves out so much detail, You remind me that the purpose of these writings is to leave a basic blueprint of the way (Your way), a summary of what You wanted us to know about how to live our lives as the Father would have us live them.

I argue here, Jesus, because in reading these more recent books, for me, You begin to emerge from that impenetrable image into a living, breathing, caring individual who can understand what day-to-day living is all about.

Jesus, as we go around giving these spiritual talks, how can we best help people to find You? How do we help them to turn their head knowledge into heart knowledge? How do we help them to feel You come alive? What is our purpose as everyday evangelizers in this present age with all its materialism, secularism, and egotism?

---

[2] a person of questionable parentage who therefore would not have been welcomed in the synagogue

You, as a disadvantaged, itinerant teacher, changed several thousand years of belief and attitude in just three years of work, and it continues today. Lord, what do You need us to do or say to help achieve Your intended goal? The pen is Yours.

☙

GG Annie, you are feeling inadequate this morning and not up to the task of working collaboratively with Me in this dialogue. You are feeling overwhelmed by concern for your children and your grandchildren. You are experiencing some concern over finances now that Bert is retired. How much longer will the old car hold out? What if the furnace breaks down and so on? Your inability to console your grandson after his parents went out for a short while last night left you feeling inadequate. Need I say more? How could you possibly be of use to Me when even your memory is beginning to let you down these days? I need you, Ann, as I need each and every one of you to live out your lives on a daily basis. This means literally staying focused on the moment.

Right now, you are doing your very best to write down as accurately as you are able that which you believe I am dictating to you. Stay focused on this. This is the work of this moment. It need not be affected by any of your concerns expressed earlier, or you do not feel confident as to how to go about getting another book published, another random thought that has just popped into your head.

You have started this communication by asking Me a question about how to bring others to Me. How can you convince others that there is a trustworthy, caring God just wanting to be befriended?

For you, Annie, your greatest selling feature is your understanding of how perfectly I have used the circumstances of your life to assist you in arriving here at this very moment. You are a good salesperson because you have come to love what you sell, Me.

You learned acceptance years ago, and once a person learns to accept what turns up on his or her plate (which does not mean that he or she has to like it), it is much easier for Us to guide them toward their goal. You have learned to look to Us for guidance as each situation—good and not so good—crops up. This is what I ask you to share as I lead you out into various situations.

You need only be conscious of what you sense we would like you to say, for you cannot force others to hear you or to accept what you say. Only I can open the hearts and minds of those who happen to hear you.

It is the same for all of you. You cannot force someone to accept Me. That is something that happens deep within a person's soul. That is strictly between this person and Me. It is the one true freedom, for it is about the only thing given freely to man that can never be taken away. It is your greatest treasure. It costs you nothing. It is freely given, and yet for many, it is so hard to find. The secret to finding it is wanting it enough so you will put aside your doubts, angers, and passions long enough to turn to Me and accept it.

So many of you give up in frustration because you come looking for a quick fix, a withdrawal of symptoms, an erasure of circumstances, a feeling! But I am not a feeling! I am a reality! I am part of you. When you breathe, I breathe. When you laugh, I laugh. When you cry, I cry. Your reality is My reality. You are not just a feeling, so how can I be just a feeling?

This scribe is so concerned at this moment that she cannot hear Me well enough to put exactly the right words down on this paper to get this message across. She alone cannot, but together We can. Her words alone will do little but scatter seeds on stony ground, but with My help, the stony ground of each soul who reads or hears these words will be transformed into fertile soil, providing that that soul wishes to be transformed. I will not change that which does not wish to be altered. I will not barge in where I am not welcome. I will not override anyone's God-given freedom to choose My Way or not.

This is a very serious point here! We are talking freedom of choice here! Remember, it is not freedom of choice if there are no alternatives. It is not freedom of choice if only one choice is acceptable. If to choose other is considered a punishable act, then where is the freedom?

Many of you perceive the outcome of living life your way as God's punishment. If things don't work out the way you wanted them to, you figure it's Me getting even for not choosing Me or My Way.

Not! (As your present lingo expresses it.)

Whether you choose My Way or your way (the highway), life will have its ups and downs. Each life is unique and should not be compared to another. Each life is a one-time story that is being written as it is being lived out. The person is the writer, and he or she gets to decide the outcome. He or she either decides to write about a hero or someone who sits back and lets circumstances of life overwhelm them.

That is why I came to earth in the form of the Christ. I came so you would have a real example of how one disadvantaged human being could turn all the circumstances of His life into a worthwhile outcome, not only for Himself but for others. He is not the only example of this, but how could I, God, ask this of My children (all of you) if I had not done it Myself? Been there! Done that! (There are some very interesting expressions in English. We'll have to get skilled translators when we have this published in other languages.)

I came so you could all have life in abundance. I said it when I was on earth, and I say it today. I came to give you life that has value. Would you please at least give this some thought? For Me to be able to give, I need you to be willing to receive.

This is Me (God) loving you, the reader of this book, at this very moment!

God O-O

WHAT SORT OF AN ATTITUDE DO I BRING TO THE TABLE?

G I'll do the talking this morning, little one. *Recent conversations and circumstances have caused you to judge your life as boring and lackluster. You see yourself as being there for others, even when you would dearly love for someone to do for you. You are seeing others as having done all sorts of exciting things, going to all sorts of exotic places, and having any number of amusing anecdotes with which to entertain companions. You feel that all you have are others' stories heard over your years of listening and seldom doing.*

You looked at your granddaughter this morning as she was dressed in a pale blue outfit and white sandals, and you thought how pretty she looked with her short blonde hair and blue eyes. You told her so, and then your eyes welled up as you tried to remember when anyone ever noticed you as a child, let alone gave you a compliment or hug.

You notice the freedom with which your husband does his thing without considering the possibility that it might conflict with your schedule. You are aware of periodic purchases that are made without checking on the availability of funds on that particular month. It's not a lot, but it adds up.

You feel that these thoughts sound like self-pity, and you learned a long time ago that self-pity is a dead end street. Now you want to know what to do with these thoughts, which, if entertained, will be unproductive in building the kingdom. I know other things are on your mind, but you are not prepared at this time to reflect openly. That's allowed.

To begin with, being aware of your thoughts and feelings is not self-pity. It is self-awareness. You cannot and will not grow if you do not know yourself. Some thoughts will create certain feelings, and feelings in themselves are neither right nor wrong. They just are. The feeling is involuntary, so therefore no judgment should be placed on it. What you do with the feeling and the accompanying thoughts is the area in which to be alert, for in this area, you do have the ability to choose your reaction and behavior.

You always have the choice of embracing the initial feeling and fertilizing it with victim thoughts or recognizing that feeling for what it is and taking the responsibility for how you can turn it into a positive outcome. For example, you are feeling dissatisfied with yourself because your weight has crept up again. Are you going to assuage your dissatisfaction and failure thoughts with a couple of cookies here or a small bowl of ice cream there? Or do you remind yourself that you are perfectly able to lose whatever amount of weight you wish to lose just by eating less and only when you are hungry? You know it works. What are you going to choose?

For example, you have an ongoing concern that you might not have enough money for the inevitable emergency. You are retired now, and as many folks would confirm, you cannot spend as freely as once you did when full salaries were the reality. You, as the bill payer, have the responsibility to alert the company of the need to spend effectively or at least only after some deliberation among yourselves.

You have been told that I will look after your needs, even making sure you have some extra from time to time to help the less fortunate. I think we did a pretty neat job of covering your property taxes this month. Did we not, Ann? This is definitely an exercise in learning to trust us. Watch as apparently insurmountable expenses are smoothly dealt with. By all means, try to keep some buffer money in the bank, but do not be afraid to use it, if need be, for you will get some months in which you will be able to replenish it. We are telling you not to worry about finances. You now have the choice to worry or not!

For example, others seem to be going places and doing things while your life seems to be pretty much humdrum. Would you believe that there are others who would give anything to have a life like yours? Most people would be able to be most satisfied with their lot if they were not always comparing it to what others have. That is one of the most destructive human failings, envy! This world's cultures and religions have produced a great number of adages about being thankful for what you have, yet so few understand the startling wisdom inherent within them.

Yes, your life right now is quite quiet in relation to some, but that could change. Anything is possible if you desire a change, express that desire to us, and leave it in our capable hands. Again the attitudinal approach is a choice you are able and responsible to make.

And above all else, we ask you to be there for others. No preoccupation of your own should so fully monopolize your thoughts to such a degree that you cannot hear or be aware of the needs of a fellow journeyer, be he or she family, friend, or a passing stranger.

Always be looking for us in others. Be attentive to the chance meeting wherever you might find yourself. The purpose of life is to live each moment, however boring or exciting, to the very best of your ability, knowing that together we can hasten the arrival of the kingdom here on earth.

Your agent in love,

God O-O

HOW TO HEAR GOD

*D*ear God, how does one get to hear You?

◊

Good question! I was wondering how long it would be before you realized that I would answer that question for you. Each time someone has complained, "I don't hear anything," I thought for sure you would think of asking Me. Thank God for Madeline's comment yesterday.

◊

Thank You, God, for Madeline's comment yesterday. I ask for the ability to write down what You say, clearly and definitively.

◊

Annie, write this.

GG There is no one sure way to hear God. Now hold on! Don't heave the book across the room in frustration and self-doubt! All We're saying is that a person's way of hearing Us is going to be uniquely suited to them. You, Ann, hear Us as if we were all in a room together, talking as friends, but you do not hear with the ears of your body. You hear with the ears of your heart. And you have been given this ability (not that you asked for it) to enable you to inscribe Our words of love for yourself and others, thus enabling Us to encourage those who are as yet unaware of their own ability to hear. Yes, all people have the potential to hear Us, yet in your modern, technological, and skeptical world, there are not many willing to take the time to hone this skill even if they knew it was available to them.

Many have walked away from Us because a church did not provide them with what they felt they needed. Now many keep themselves so busy that they just distract themselves from the still, quiet voice of the inner spirit, wishing to be acknowledged. Most no longer recognize the source of their discontent, yet the awareness of that discontent is pure gift. Only when a person realizes that nothing on earth will satisfy that mysterious longing will he or she start to search for other, and that other is Us.

First, there must be the desire, need, and openness to discover the true meaning and purpose of life. Once the desire has been seeded, then any number of channels will become apparent to the searcher. Many who have heard from others that a person can hear God will sit for a while listening, but when nothing extraordinary is forthcoming, they give up. If all one is expecting is to hear Me, without any desire to know or love Me, he or she probably can understand why he or she does not hear Me.

If all a person wants from a relationship with Me is to have Me fix whatever is wrong in their life, they should be able to understand why they do not hear Me. If they truly want a relationship with Me, which will require time and patience, then they can expect to begin to feel listened to by Me, heard by Me, and loved by Me. The person will imperceptibly begin to realize that they actually feel that they love Me in return, and in various, changing, and ever-perfecting ways, they will know that they hear Me.

I will meet all souls just where they are, with all their faults, shortcomings, and limitations. No one is prohibited from finding Me. Some come looking for Me only when they feel they need Me. Others want to hear only what they want to hear. A few are afraid to hear what they think I would say if they truly listened. They would not be afraid if they truly knew Me!

If you have no friends, come to Me, and I will teach you how to be a friend to Me and others. If you have fair-weather friends, come to Me, and I will teach you of meaningful friendship with Me and others. If you are fortunate enough to have trustworthy friends, come to Me, and I will astound you with the infiniteness of My love for you and all others.

Do you truly wish to hear God? First learn who I am through My Son Jesus. "If you know Me, you know the Father" (John 14: 7). Be prepared to read books that seem to be presented to you or seem to attract your attention. Read scripture. Talk to Me, and then be silent, giving yourself the opportunity to practice listening. Ask Me for what you need, expecting Me to meet your needs and accepting the outcome. Know that, whatever the outcome is, it will give you the perfect opportunity to grow wiser and more knowledgeable because you opened yourself up to learning.

I am not an easy ticket to what you think will make you happy, but I am an exceedingly wise travelling companion who knows how to handle any challenge along our journey. I am able to facilitate sudden curves when necessary and will give you the assurance that you can handle anything that we might encounter as long as you are open to the experience.

Life is not easy for anyone, but the journey is much less difficult if you walk with Me and listen to My suggestions. Anyone will be able to hear Me if he or she desires to. I search out that desire in hearts.

God 0-0

LIVING IN FEAR OR LIVING IN LOVE

*D*ear God, for some time now, You have been stressing Your infinite love, compassion, and forgiveness. Now this morning I read Matthew 3:7–12 where John the Baptist is calling the Pharisees and Sadducees "a group of vipers" and goes on to talk of change or the chaff will be burned in unquenchable fire.

Lord, You speak to me of nothing but love, assuring me that I have free choice to do something that is not exactly perfect or brilliant. You can work with that. You have allowed this message of unquenchable fire to persist in scripture for two thousand years. How could what You seem to be whispering softly to me also be right? I am an unworldly housewife. Am I deluding myself? Is it the devil in the woman? Am I looking at life through rose-colored glasses? What should I come to understand with God glasses?

○3

GG Ann, thank you for addressing this question. It is one that surfaces continually to haunt the inner depths of a soul. I know what your religion has taught you, and I know it did so with the most well-meaning intentions, but the kingdom is at hand, and it is time to embrace the kingdom to bring it to earth in all its glory.

Remember, John the Baptist was a human, filled with a spirit that showed him the imperfections of life as it was being lived then. He saw the emptiness of ritual for the sake of ritual, rules, and regulations that served man, not God, and a people who struggled under the yoke of oppression, not only Roman but a religious hierarchy. He was not speaking to the lowly and brokenhearted (Isa. 61). When he threatened unquenchable fire, he was using threatening language to shake very powerful people out of their blindness to the unloving practices of their society.

As you all know, threats are a last resort of a loving parent who struggles to allow a self-willed child to continue learning the hard way. No parent wants to see his or her offspring suffer, let alone unnecessarily. If a little fear keeps some from making dire decisions, it's all well and good. But let us not leave it there.

Like all parent/child relationships, the parent, who has hopefully transmitted some basic dos and don'ts (just to reduce experimentation with its potential dangers) knows that, as the child matures, they will see for themselves the wisdom of the original rules and come to understand that threats were necessary during that period when they had no wisdom of their own. With maturity comes understanding and the development of a relationship based on love and respect. Fear becomes a thing of the past, and acquiescence (obedience) becomes the path of choice, not because it is demanded but because you choose it willingly.

It is the same with you and I. Fear can have its place when a soul is young and unformed. As it matures and grows in relationship with Me, it learns My mandates and looks only there when it needs to choose a way to go. Only those who do not truly know Me behave in an unloving manner, and if they do not know Me, how can you, who do know Me, fault them for their unknowing behavior?

So I say to you, "Come and spend time with me. Get to know Me and My ways. Spend less time in fear of evil, for time spent in fear is time not spent in My love in My kingdom." I bring peace, and I give My peace to you. Let Me speak directly to your heart. Allow yourself to mature spiritually. Stop expecting perfection from a church made up of people like you. That church can be only as perfect as you are. Perfect yourselves, and churches will perfect, becoming more loving, compassionate, and forgiving. As you allow your heart to become more open to My love for you, your love for Me will grow. The next thing you know, you will start to care for yourself and others, and only God knows where that could lead!

Love? Unity? Oneness? The kingdom here on earth! I love you so very much.

God O-O

DOES SATAN EXIST?

Dear God, This morning I read Matthew 4, the temptation.

☙

GG Annie, you wrestle with the question, "Is there really a personified evil in the form of Satan?" How would it be if I express it this way? Evil exists because I exist. Evil must exist so that those who are My followers and those who search for Me are able to find Me. To find Me, you have to know how to recognize Me, and to recognize Me, you must know what I am and what I am not. For Me to be defined as all good, you need to be able to recognize that which is not all good. For you to know what love is, you must come to know what love is not.

There can be no understanding of up and down if all is on one level. There can be no experience of hot if a person has never experienced cool. Why would anyone turn to Me unless he or she sees Me as other than the rest? A person or thing can be described by that which it is not, so therefore My infinite goodness and love could only be comprehended if there existed in this world that which is not infinite goodness and love.

Is there actually an evil spirit that has come to be called Satan, or does evil merely live in the hearts of mankind to varying degrees? Does personifying evil make it easier to tolerate one's shortcomings by being able to put the blame elsewhere as in, "The devil made me do it"?

If personifying evil helps to keep you alert to it, then it serves you and Me. If personifying evil keeps you more focused on the fear of evil than on the loving good, it is distracting you from drawing closer to Me in love and friendship. Ask Me to instruct you, and follow the dictates I will present to your heart.

The ways in which Jesus was tempted are the ways in which all humans are tempted—through needs, greed, and My stipulation that the quality of humility be ever present in each and every one of you.

I tell you that I will meet your needs. I suffer your greed. I will reward your deeds done with humility.[3]

O-O

---

[3] Please make every effort to appreciate the vast difference between humility and humiliation. Many confuse these terms, thinking that, to be humble, one must become a doormat. Follow the example of Jesus. He was humble but not a doormat. For those of you saying, "Ya and He got himself crucified by His humility," always remember that He allowed it!

MARITAL DIFFICULTIES

*D*ear God, Three people who are close to me are going through marital difficulties these days, and each calls me from time to time to talk. Lord, I hardly feel qualified to be giving input in situations like these, let alone counseling, but as there is some common ground here and this is a universal problem, do You have some wisdom that You would like included in this book? The world certainly has its opinions and advice on infidelity, loss of intimacy, outgrowing of relationships, and so on, but how do they appear through Your eyes?

ଔ

GG Annie, write this. For those whose marriages appear to be deteriorating, are you wondering where it went wrong or how you can cope with another affair? Are you trying to make up your mind to put an end to it? Are you so angry that all you want to do is get even, that is, you want them to hurt as much as you do? Are your self-loathing and shame so great that you cannot see beyond them? Does it feel as though your whole world is falling apart? Sit down, put up your feet, and take a few really deep breaths. Let's talk!

Several sets of circumstances will fit into this theme, and we will deal with a few of the more obvious ones. For those whose circumstances do not match the text exactly, you will probably find some common threads to which you can relate.

Regardless of how you learned to view marriage, be it a sacred covenant between both of you and Me, a legal must, or a feeling that you had to, it is one of the most difficult forms of human relationship to keep in good working order. Any relationship initially based on emotions will naturally be more fragile than one created by a contractual format. Under a contract, the rules are clear. Each party agrees to provide certain goods or services while acknowledging certain consequences for failure to do so.

In marriage, no such clarity exists. Each person goes into the relationship with unspoken expectations and hopes. Seldom does each person keep a running inventory of those that are met, but all too often, he or she remembers those that are not met. This might be the experience of each of the partners, yet each one somehow is only able to be cognizant of their own list of disappointments. Furthermore, in a contract, the termination of dealings with each other is clear. As long as each side fulfills their agreed obligation either to quality, service, or duration, they are usually free to terminate the contract on an agreed date. Each party is free to renegotiate or look elsewhere.

This is not the way you humans have designed or defined marital relationships, certainly not those of you who profess to include Me in the covenant. You enter the relationship for various reasons. Sexual attraction is a major drawing card, mutual interest is another, and "he or she meets my needs" probably covers a lot. Do you notice that I have not mentioned the word love here? I have done this intentionally, for love means different things to different people.

People use this word so loosely today that I'm not surprised when you wake up some morning thinking you have lost it. The word has so many meanings that you are hard pressed to know just what you have lost. For example, people say, "I love apple pie! I love climbing mountains, reading a good book, or listening to music." They also might say that they love running, wearing a particular piece of clothing, smelling lavender, or seeing a sunset. You also love your pets. Do you begin to see how foggy your definition of love is or how a person's definition of love might be all caught up in feelings? And if the feelings are not making you feel good, then maybe the love is gone!?

A young couple may exchange "I love you" after a sexual encounter. Another couple may say "I love you" as they realize they both enjoy a particular activity such as sightseeing, a concert, reading, or a quiet dinner. Another couple is all aglow after a wonderful evening with others. They loved how each other looked, danced, spoke, and acted. They also loved how they felt when their partner made them feel beautiful or handsome while looking them in the eyes and expressing it.

As time passes and circumstances change, partners may not always project that sought-after feeling when life's more difficult moments distract them. Should circumstances cause this situation to persist, the feelings may no longer be projected, and feelings of not being loved might start to surface. I think most of you can see where this might lead, and I'm also hoping you are getting a clearer picture of the weakness of your comprehension of the word love. Unfortunately that weakness is often the foundation of so many of your marriages.

Now I am not saying that feelings should not be part of your decision making when it comes to marriage. As a matter of fact, it is a very reasonable beginning! You all have to learn to walk before you can run. In fact, most of the choices you make in your lifetime will have some element of feeling involved in it.

A child who is being berated by his parent for having infringed on one of his family's rules does not feel particularly loved at that precise moment, but if he knows he deserves the censure, it will not undermine his sense of being loved. His sense of being loved is not a feeling. It is a knowing.

Feelings are not love! True love is unconditional! Unconditional love is God's love. It has no conditions, stipulations, riders, ifs, ands, or buts. It has no reason for termination. It just is. You can find it in the most unlikely people and the most unusual circumstances. It is also something that one chooses to do in spite of one's own feelings despite another's behavior. It transcends anything put in its way. Love changes everything!

God O-O

WHAT IS NEEDED FOR A LASTING MARRIAGE

Papa, the pain continues for the three people I know and all people around the world who are experiencing marital discord. Are You asking me to write this morning?

☙

Yes, Ann, I am.

GG *You sense one attitude of loss of interest. You hear another who is willing to endure the unacceptable so as not to be alone. You listened last evening to the words of the third who has grown so much through these painful episodes that now, as another begins, she is able to say, "Just go. Do what you feel you need to do, but do not expect me to enable you or to accept the blame you wish to heap upon me to give your conscience an excuse or legitimate reason for leaving." There are so many other stories and circumstances, Ann, but most could be ultimately described as a change of heart.*

What is a change of heart? It is a turning away from. People quite often express it as, "I've changed my mind." Good relationships are built on like-mindedness. Certain characteristics in one person are attractive to the other person and vice versa. Friendships, marriages, business partnerships, and so forth are all built on one party being able to appreciate particular qualities inherent in the other. Sometimes one quality is so attractive to another person that it blinds him or her to other less attractive aspects of that person's character. A person who likes or needs the power and security of money will search out a person who appears to have the ability to amass money. Sometimes that need is so strong that it blinds him or her to other inherent qualities that might eventually make that partner a difficult choice for a long-term relationship.

In a marital relationship, being physically attracted to another is only the beginning, and as everyone knows, being physically attracted to another is not just limited to the married state. This is why wisdom suggests a period of getting to know someone well before making any commitment. Once attracted to someone, there are decisions to make. Many today jump right into the sexual pleasure with all the inherent problems that may produce. Another choice could be to acknowledge the attraction but make the effort to keep that low-key until you have familiarized yourself with the more in-depth aspects of this potential partner.

Sexuality is powerful for a reason. Mankind would be hard-pressed to commit to the difficult work of relationship building without it. Anyone who has been married long enough for the excitement of sexual intercourse with the original partner to cool somewhat will know exactly what is being said here. When sexual intercourse is no longer the first and last order of the day, the true character of the partners begins to become distinct. It is then that one comes to appreciate that the relationship was based on more than just sexual attraction.

Partnership is also a great opportunity for growth. Any kind of interpersonal relationship will create a potential for personal growth, but the marital relationship is one of the most demanding. It holds the greatest number of breaking points because it is a 24/7/365 commitment. There is no breather, no time-out, or no recess.

It is formed around trust (spoken and unspoken), expectations (verbal and nonverbal [a major potential pitfall]), intimacy, strengths and weaknesses, and physical attraction, which ebb and flow due to hormones, age, and health, mental or physical. It is also affected by the maturity of each partner and the openness of each to accept growth in oneself and the other.

Have you noticed that the word love has not yet been uttered?

God 0-0

UNCONDITIONAL LOVE

What is love, God? What is love from Your perspective? What should we be aiming for?

☙

Ann,

GG Aim for unconditional love, and then seek even better manifestations of it as you see yourselves falling short of the mark. Confusing? I'll try to clarify.

I love you all unconditionally, which means that, no matter what you do, I love you. That does not mean that I like all you do, think, or say, but I created you, and I know your potential. And that is loveable.

You have an expression, "God does not make junk." It may appear to be just a cute little statement, but it carries a weighty truth. Nothing I create is without value, and humans are My most satisfying creation to date.

Each of you is a little bit of Me, whether you believe that or not. And because of this, I care deeply about your welfare. You can do nothing to cause Me to lose interest in you. That is unconditional love. Those of you who have been responsible in any way for guiding others (parents, guardians, teachers, and so forth) will understand this idea more easily.

When you love unconditionally, you give another the freedom to grow. In the beginning, you may set some ground rules appropriate to the individual involved, but as each grows, the rules become patterns of behavior, accepted out of love for the other, no longer adhered to in obedience to another's demands. Sometimes the rules or expectations are not met or may be disregarded. Does that cause you to cease to care, to feel, or to love? It should not with you, and it certainly does not with Me.

You may have breaking points, that being the point at which certain behavior is believed to be no longer acceptable or forgivable. I do not experience breaking points. I always accept you where you are, and you are always forgiven, regardless of the circumstances, and it hinges on your desire for My forgiveness.

If a person does not desire or want My forgiveness, there is not much point in My giving it, is there? This is unconditional love. The forgiveness is always there. You need only to desire it. Unconditional love then gives the person the freedom to grow beyond where he or she has been, to leave behind the old self and its shortcomings and brokenness. It gives the individual the opportunity to discover more of one's true self.

Regarding relational situations, you may be beginning to perceive why so many marriages seem to be breaking down these days. They are not grounded in unconditional love. They are grounded in unrealistic expectations and very conditional love. For example:

- *"I will love you as long as you—"*
- *"I expect you to love me as I am, but there are some things about you that I am beginning to find unacceptable."*
- *"Now that we are married, you should not be spending as much time with your friends."*
- *"I expect you to love me as I change, but I have the right to decide just how you are to change."*

As the world discovers ever better ways to eradicate pain, stay healthier, live longer, and make life easier and more fun-filled, it has blinded itself to the reality and true purpose of life. Life is a journey to be experienced fully, the good and not so good. It all has purpose and the potential to help you to grow emotionally and, ultimately, spiritually. **You are all spiritual beings, and life manifests in abundance when that reality becomes understood and utilized.**

So what is unconditional love? It can be seen as an acceptance of where you are and where someone else is; the allowing of someone to grow or stay where they are until they see that they need to grow; or the understanding that unconditional love has no conditions.

Now take all the "Yes buts" that come to mind and present them to Me, and I will help you to weigh them carefully. And between us, we will work out a plan of action that will allow all parties involved to grow at their required pace.

You need only want to. I can do the rest.

God 0-0

TREATING OTHERS AS YOU WOULD LIKE THEM TO TREAT YOU

*D*ear God, yesterday was a real eye-opener, and I want to thank You. I went off to the market with Nadia, a fruit-growing friend who needed an extra set of hands to help out. As is my want, I was anxious about not getting up on time, doing the driving (seventy kilometers on the highway), maintaining my energy levels, and having the ability to know what to do. I also wanted to not just be in the way, as I am a nonfarming sort. I also worried about my back, the leg that swells, and so forth.

You got me up before the alarm went off. My preparations were not rushed. I got away on time and picked up my passenger, Stephanus, obviously a good friend of Yours. We share similarities in our journeys.

I seemed to be able to pick up what had to be done in setting up. Making change was easy, and I enjoyed the amazing variety of people who came by. I remained calm in the heavy traffic coming out of Toronto and through a torrential downpour that started as we headed east again, back into the Niagara Peninsula.

When we arrived at the parking lot where Stephanus had left his car for the day, a sea of water met us everywhere. We were exhausted and decided to treat ourselves to a hot drink together at a nearby coffee shop. We happily plodded through the water, which soothed our hot, tired feet as it filled our shoes. The rain cooled our faces, and I was surprised at the wonderful freeing feeling I was experiencing. This uptight, stuffy city person felt great!

I got home safely. I had survived. My back had held up, and my ankle was less swollen than on a busy day at home. This day, which I am beginning to think was one that You choreographed, had given me a new sense of self, hope, and self-respect. I had a modicum of ability as opposed to feelings of ineptitude.

Thank You, God!

....

Annie, I am glad that you enjoyed yourself, but I would like for you to see even more deeply into the experience and document the findings.

GG *The most obvious awareness for you was to discover that you were not afraid behind the wheel. Because you drive infrequently these days and because your style of handling a car is different than Bert's (as he drives more aggressively), you have come to dismiss your ability because it is not the same as someone else's. Each person is an individual with unique characteristics and style. No two people do anything exactly the same way. If your way of doing something achieves the same results as another's, why would a difference diminish the worth of either?*

Learn to be grateful to Me for who and what you are becoming. Cease measuring yourself with other peoples' yardsticks. I created you all as unique individuals. Why are you such slaves to uniformity?

Another awareness with which you were gifted was that of Stephanus' spiritual journey. You have felt so alone in your own journey, for you have not run into too many people who have an intimate relationship with Me, one that allows them to cut loose from the limitations of institutional religion. You felt encouraged in hearing that another soul also feels comfortable coming directly to Me, asking for My input, and obtaining My peace without needing to follow a predetermined formula of words.

The church is supposed to be My body, a community of people who reflect My love. It was never intended to appear, at times, as an unapproachable and judgmental enclave of dispassionate lawmakers who have very little comprehension or compassion for the average human being.

The purpose of life on earth is to find My purpose for you, to develop a close friendship with Me, and to serve the cause, to establish My kingdom here on earth. To know, love, and serve God, to put it in more familiar words.

To know Me means virtually what it means to know a friend. Yes, you can get to know Me that well, and anyone and everyone is invited to do so. If someone truly wishes to get to know Me and proves it with persistence, I will reward them abundantly. If a person chooses to remain where they are—comfortable, familiar, and unchallenged—then I will respect that choice. I force Myself upon no one, but I do call every soul to an ever-deepening companionship with Me.

Another awareness I would like highlighted is that of "an honest wage for an honest day's work." Your friendship with Nadia and her family has made you aware of the amount of work that goes into growing, harvesting, and marketing quality fruits and vegetables. You see the long hours, the exhausting physical work, and the potentially devastating outcome of too much or too little rain, sun, cold, and heat, to say nothing of insects, animals, and birds.

You see the fragility of the product and the importance of getting it to market at just the right time. You know they work late into the evening to pack the truck with the produce (which took all day to sort and box) as well as all else they might need for the following day. You were all up and on the road long before dawn so as to be set up and ready for business when the market opened at eight. All this work and still no money had been earned!

As you notice throughout the day, Nadia is obviously well respected by those who know her and the quality of her produce. One does not find spoiled produce under a top layer of "buy me" quality product. She is an honest woman, and she has worked harder than many for what she has achieved.

A customer approached you, looked at the sign that told the asking price, and then asked you, "How much?" You responded with the price on the sign, which was $3.50 per basket. To which she responded, "Will you take three?"

There are those of you who feel that making or saving a dollar is more important than giving full measure for full measure. Your maturing social awareness abolished slavery years ago, yet surreptitiously, it has been reestablished in your present-day sweat shops and Third World manufacturing locations where inadequate wages are paid to many so a few may live affluently.

You may think that you cannot change the world, but you can change how you treat the world. You are able to change your attitudes, and you know full well that, if you all changed your attitudes toward one another, the world would automatically change. You are asked only to be accountable for your own actions. I can handle the rest.

Go now, but stay alert to appreciating and loving who you truly are and who I truly am. And be conscious of how you treat others. I think I've mentioned this at least once before. Treat others as you would have them treat you.

I love you all—you and you and you.

God O-O

9/11

*D*ear God, we are in shock! As best we know, isolated up here on the French River, a group of Muslim fundamentalists has hijacked seven passenger planes, and all but two have been blown out of the sky or smashed into skyscrapers or other important buildings in New York City. Borders between us and the States have been closed, as have most airports.

Lord, the pen is Yours. I sensed that You tapped me on the shoulder a little while ago. If so, I am at Your disposal. We four, so far removed from the devastation, know we need to hear and feel You and sense Your comforting presence. How much more are those directly affected needing You and Your wisdom at this moment!

☙

Annie, my Annie, write this.

GG You are all My children, whether some of you wish to hear this or not. When this material goes to print, some of those who have been directly affected by today's events will still be frozen in time, unable to move beyond the pain, anguish, terror, anger, hatred, and accompanying desire for revenge. I tell you this: The intensity of these emotions will find a parallel in the intensity of the emotions of those who carried out these acts against all of mankind and Me and all I am.

As you can all see at this very moment, anger and resentment, if left unaddressed, have the ability to lead any one of you to commit criminal acts of violence, cruelty, or self-destruction that, under ordinary circumstances, would never remotely be considered.

Yes, you might go into shock when faced with loss, extreme pain (either physical or emotional), the diagnosis of a terminal illness, or anything that shatters the normal routine of your everyday life. This is often the body's protective response to real or perceived disaster, and it can serve you well temporarily. Eventually you will be expected to face the reality of what has occurred and to work through it to resolution. If this does not happen, that anger, resentment, or lack of forgiveness can take seed, leading to a cancerous growth. Be that growth an actual tumor or an emotional derailment, that unresolved issue could eat away at your humanity, leaving you an empty shell, dead to life, or alive to cause death.

As always, the choice is up to each individual. Does the person choose life or decide to allow all that is his or her potential to decay, erasing all redeeming purpose for his or her very existence? Do you find these harsh words? If yes, maybe it is because they jar you out of a feeling of righteous anger—anger at others, anger at yourself, or anger at Me. No one is exempt from gleaning some directive in this communication. Each of you has found justification at one time or another for some word or action that you chose to say or do in response to another's behavior.

Yes, most assuredly, there are varying degrees of evil, but they are all still ungodly. If your ungodly behaviors do not include murder and mayhem, it means you are not one of the more broken among you. Be grateful! There are many among you who, whether intentionally or inadvertently, have come to realize that they are living in a hell right here on earth.

I do not ask anyone to change the world. I do not ask more of you than you are capable of giving. I do ask that you become willing to consider life over death. I will not force you to change, but I will work with you nonstop if you but ask for My help. I never leave. Only you turn your back to Me. The farther you distance yourself from all I am, the closer you come to all I am not! That which has happened today was done by those who have rejected all I am.

Where do you stand? Are you miles away? Do you stand with your back to Me? Any behavior, whether significant or not so, if not of Me, is not of Me! There is always a first step that eventually leads to any action, however vile. If you wish to change the world, to eradicate evil to assist at the heralding in of My kingdom here on earth, then you must begin with the house cleaning in your personal world. My kingdom will come. You decide how quickly.

Do not be disheartened. I still work miracles (quite often with your help). I am still omnipotent, omniscient, and omnipresent, and I am still able to extract gold from what might appear to be dross. If evil seems powerful, it is because some of you have made a place for it in your hearts. Each of you can quite easily counterbalance this by making more room for Me in your heart and less space for angry and vengeful thoughts. Trust Me! You do your part, and I will do the rest. Watch as we work to extract the gold from that which appears to have no possible value.

Your Creator, your Counsel, your Comforter, and your friend,

0-0

REACTION VERSUS PROACTION

You nudged, Lord? The pen is Yours.

ଔ

Thank you, Ann. Write this.

GG So many of you are experiencing feelings of vulnerability, feelings with which possibly you are not all that familiar. You in North America have not seen acts of war happening before your very eyes in your own country. To date, war was something that happened there, not here at home.

This scribe's pen halted momentarily when I used the word war, but I use this word for it typifies any situation where meaningful dialogue is no longer being pursued. Demands and threats become the next stage in the development. All-out war occurs when egos get too big, when one side feels it is justified in forcing its way upon someone else. I do not force My way upon any one of you. Why do you force anything upon anyone else?

This communication is not speaking of armed conflict, but it makes a good analogy, for many of you attempt to achieve your own ends by the most unloving methods. Simply put, when someone does something to you that you do not like, you cannot but react internally. Yet how you react externally becomes the definition of who you are and how you wish to be perceived.

If you retaliate with like kind, you parallel yourself to the level of the initial aggression. If you are never the aggressor but will always hit back when attacked, then you are only slightly more advanced than the aggressor. If it takes an awful lot to cause you to overtly react, you are beginning to grow in maturity. If violence is never your way but you resolve issues with eventual withdrawal of privileges or self, you might be called a peacekeeper but not always loving. If you bring all your concerns to Me and ask My advice as to what your reaction should be, then you are functioning in enlightenment.

There is not one formula for dealing with others, for everyone is unique and requires individual handling. Know the enemy, whether it resides in others or yourself. Learn to recognize when your ego is speaking more loudly than My wisdom, which is available to you all if only you would take the time to listen.

I am not saying that My Way is the easiest. In actuality, it is often the hardest, yet when an event is over, it produces the finest results and is ever reducing the incidence of repetition. I say to you, "Don't be afraid!" Many of you are quite filled with fear on a regular basis, let alone a week or so after a major attack on the twin towers.

The Western world fears a loss of power and anything that threatens its way of life, liberty, and pursuit of happiness, which has, in most part, been pursued despite a great cry for help from other countries not as fortunate.

The bigger and more powerful you are, the more cognizant you must be of how your actions affect others. The more power you hold, the more wisdom you need. Even though power comes with many perks, it also comes with a downside arising out of the resentment felt by those who are powerless.

To hold power, you just have to be stronger than another is. To sustain power, you must wield it wisely, enabling the less powerful to feel empowered by you. This fact is truth on a personal or family level or in business, politics, education, and, most definitely, global situations. I have allowed your power. Use it wisely, or you will lose it. No, I will not take it away. But your choices, if self-serving, will eventually cause you to lose it. Power, when improperly handled, causes pockets of dissatisfaction. When improperly handled, it leads to eventual conflict, which, when improperly handled, eventually leads to the breakdown of a structure.

If you choose to act with My wisdom, you will be furthering the growth of the kingdom here on earth and your own peaceful existence. Go in peace and love to serve others.

0-0

A PARADIGM SHIFT

I'll take it from here, Ann. We've had a bit of a hiatus. I know you have been busy with the other manuscript.

GG Your thoughts have led you here this morning.

You and your group have been giving seminars in your area for three years, yet some of you feel you are making little impact. The people who you think really need to hear your presentations never show up. You get the older souls and the handful in each parish who are already spiritually alive, and your concern is that the rest of the people go on about their lives totally oblivious to all I am and all I offer. You are concerned that folks' reactions to occurrences such as September 11 could cause some to become walled in, fearful, and self-preserving, which most assuredly does not lead to kingdom building.

As you saw how poor the last turnout was at the last session, you, My scribe, were wondering if this is at all worthwhile. What is the point if the people who could best benefit from this material seldom if ever show up at the doors of the churches you are in? I'll tell you what the point is! To use one of your latest buzzwords, you are on the cutting edge of lay spiritual ministry.

For the last two thousand years, churches have depended upon their clergy to maintain a relationship with Me. Everything has been channeled through a small number of men and almost no women who lead a lifestyle that is quite different from the people they are supposedly serving. The difference is basically a lifestyle of aloneness or lack of familiarity with the everyday activities and pursuits of their flock. That flock has put all responsibility on the shoulders of its clergy for their salvation. They turn to their priests and ministers for all advice, and as a result, very few know who or what I am and all I offer.

Many of you are still caught in the belief system that teaches that, when you follow a formula of prayers and routine rituals, you will achieve eternal life. Some of you believe that the key to opening the gates of heaven for yourself is to acknowledge that Jesus died for you. Period. Nothing else is relevant. "You've been saved." But saved from what?

Many who call themselves My followers are so caught up in a preoccupation with sin and punishment that they never experience the fullness of life. They do not grow beyond the childlike belief that, if they do something they believe to be wrong and get caught, they will be punished.

Seeing as how, as humans, you are most likely on occasion to behave in a manner that could use some enlightenment and knowing I probably don't miss much, do you really feel that it is productive to think of Me as sitting around keeping a record of your failings? Might there be a more mature attitude that befits the precious offspring of a loving God? Do you expect your adult children to still follow, to the letter, all you taught them as they were growing up? Do you extract that obedience with fear tactics, demeaning behavior, or comments? Do you turn your backs on the children who do not follow your advice to the letter?

I do not use any of the above tactics, for I give all of you the freedom to handle your lives in whatever manner you might choose. Some choices are wiser than others are, but I do not butt in unless I am invited or unless one of your choices has no redeeming outcome.

In most instances, all of you are given the freedom to live and respond to your lives in whatever manner you choose. Notice that I use the word respond. This is a key word. Most of you will live pretty average lives with the periodic high or low. Your response to the highs, lows, and everyday in-betweens is much more important than the actual circumstances of those moments.

You have a very apt saying that states, "The glass is either half full or half empty." The glass is containing the same amount of content, regardless of who is looking at it, yet the perceptions are vastly different. On the one hand, the observer perceives he still has as much left as he has already enjoyed and anticipates enjoying the other half. The other observer perceives that he has already used up half of what he had, and now it's almost gone. He must be careful how he uses it, sparingly and not with enthusiasm.

Perceptions

This communication started out with a 'half-empty' perception. You, My scribe, are looking at the ratio of the number of persons who attend these sessions compared to the number of people who attend any one particular church. You, My scribe, are looking at the type of people who attend these sessions and sense that many already know a lot of what you talk about. You wonder why they keep coming back.

Annie, write this.

GG You are doing My work. I send the people to you to give you the opportunity to practice, to understand that what you are saying is feeding those who wish to hear. The fact that many return indicates you are projecting Me to those who you say already know Me, for those persons will recognize Me in you all. What more could you ask for? What better confirmation do you need? These people know, so they do not argue or give you a hard time.

Those who you feel need to hear what you have to say (and you most assuredly are right) will eventually be led to you. But for them, you will need to be seasoned, convicted enough, and able to confidently hear Me so that, when you are confronted, you not only will know the suitable response for each searcher but will also have the skill and peace to present it convincingly. These have been baby steps. You have been getting your feet wet.

For the next little while, I need each of you who feels committed to doing the work for the advancement of the kingdom to concentrate on deepening your relationship with Me. I need you to spend more time listening to your heart. I ask you to reread scripture, looking for new meaning (a grander vision for you), and to share it with each other. I am going to ask you to allow Me to present you with new reading material that will open fresh horizons for you, and I will ask you to share those findings with each other. I am going to ask you to request and leave yourselves open to the receiving of a deeper understanding of My many gifts and to prepare yourselves to receive new ones. I am going to ask you to put away the old and put on the new.

- *less judgment—more compassion*
- *less talking—more listening*
- *less church—more community*

This will be easier for some of you than others. Do not be afraid. You, of course, have the freedom to bow out, to stay where you are for as long as you feel you need to. For those of you who feel excited by this communication, know that I will be leading you every step of the way and I will give you all the time you need to get up to speed.

There is much still to impart. This is why I am asking each of you to listen, read, learn, and share, for that will take less time than if you all have to do all the lessons. This way, you can instruct each other with what I will be presenting to you individually.

It is imperative that you hone your listening skills to be more open to what each of you will be saying, for I will be presenting ideas, concepts, and perspectives that will be new to you all. I will not allow you to be misled, for it would not serve My purpose or My kingdom if you were to be.

Trust Me. Take this quiet time to sharpen your listening skills, familiarizing yourselves with My inner voice that will become your beacon, your discernment, and your joy. When you are ready and willing, we'll take on the world and invite it into the kingdom. Many churches will be able to use the assistance of these awakened people, My salt for the earth. I await your individual decisions.

0-0

LESS JUDGMENT—
MORE COMPASSION

There has been conflict and disagreement in one of the Christian churches as to how the sacrament of reconciliation is to be administered. The old method involved telling all to a priest. The more recent method is presented to anyone who wishes to participate in a group celebration.

Does the sinner who quietly slips in the open door and sits ashamedly at the back of the church during the reconciliation service receive your forgiveness, or must he or she verbalize his or her shame to another human being (minister of confession)?

☙

I'll take it from here, Annie.

GG I love all human beings! What the world calls the worst sinner has always been and will always be My most precious charge and My greatest concern, not because they are facing damnation but because they are in the greatest pain.

Only those who have walked in those footsteps can comprehend just how destructively and hopelessly a soul behaves when not only their conscience but also the community in which they live, points an accusing and shaming finger at them. The spirit might as well be nonexistent as the person's soul gasps for nourishment, and the body, equally desperate, resorts to survival tactics if it chooses to stay alive. This is an extreme example, and yet to a much less serious extent, you all experience this reality throughout your lives.

I created you all. I live in you all, regardless of the degree to which I am visible to others. To those who have never been tested beyond your means, be grateful. There are those whose life circumstances have denied them the knowledge and skills necessary to make wise decisions. You would not mock or criticize a person with a broken leg for walking with difficulty. Why do you so readily point fingers at the questionable behavior of broken souls?

A broken soul does not trust Me. A broken soul more than likely doesn't trust anyone. He will attempt to ease his discomfort with the least amount of added pain. So is it not obvious that it would be wise to hold communal celebrations for just this reason, to ease the pain and shame, to help him to carry his cross, or to allow him to learn how to forgive himself (or maybe even to learn to love himself)!

I, Christ, have already been scourged, shamed, abandoned, spat upon, impaled, and killed once and for all. I do not ask that anyone else should be so treated ever again. A person should be free to come to Me in whatever manner that will lead to his development of trust in Me. You humans have been known to be somewhat more judgmental than I am. I ask you all to leave the door ajar to allow the aching soul an opportunity to seek and obtain solace without having to reveal its brokenness to anyone except Me. In time, that soul may seek out dialogue with another trusted individual if that will increase spiritual and emotional health. I may even choose to instruct that soul Myself.

Please love and respect these precious jewels of Mine, and meet them where they are. Do not ask the crippled and the lame to run a marathon!

0-0

EXPECTATIONS

Annie, write this. You and thousands like you were let down by Christmas this year and quite often by Christmas in general. Your frustration emerged in the chaos of putting on a meal for fifteen people, trying to have everything ready and still hot all at the same time. You were disappointed that you didn't get the opportunity to watch and enjoy the reactions as your grandchildren opened their presents. Your other guests were coming in about that time, and greeting the new arrivals was also important to you.

When asked what you wanted for Christmas, you mentioned you were in need of a new wallet. Between the two of you, you received gift certificates for six different businesses, but not one of them sold wallets. You also received and probably gave many things that were not needed. So much money was spent on unnecessary things when, in actuality, you could have used the money this year. Bert's retirement and the related salary reduction have caused you quite a bit of concern these past eleven months in spite of My assurance that your every need will be met. Have your needs been met so far?

ଛ

Yes, Lord, and more!

ଛ

You were looking forward to sitting after the meal with your guests and maybe having some carol singing or just some conversation, but others were doing your dishes and asking what you wanted done with the leftovers, which required your attendance in the kitchen. By the time you felt that you could sit down, the children were getting tired and cranky, and certain others were murmuring about it being time to leave.

The best part of the day for you was when your granddaughter Emma climbed into a chair beside you as you all stood around the groaning table while your daughter Karen said Grace. Karen's words and Emma's hug brought tears to your eyes. Another special moment came when Karen was leaving. Remembering that she needed some milk, she ran back to the house to ask if we might have an extra bag. Her parting words were, "I love you!"

Annie,

GG So many of you are disappointed by Christmas. You are disappointed because your expectations or what the world says your expectations should or could be are not realized. Maybe the answer lies in changing your expectations.

Example A

First expectation: I want this meal to be perfect without any glitches.

Altered expectation: I want everyone to have a special meal, a warm (if not hot), well-cooked, tasty, filling meal.

Was the second expectation met, Ann?

ଓଃ

I believe it was, Lord.

ଓଃ

Example B

First expectation: *I want to see my grandchildren open the presents we bought for them so I could feel good about the purchases and see their excitement.*

Altered expectation: *I want my grandchildren to get pleasure out of my choice of gifts for them. Their continued attention to these gifts during the evening would assure me of this.*

Was the second expectation met, Annie?

༄

Yes, Lord.

༄

Example C

First expectation: *I want to please people with the gifts I give.*

This is probably everyone's hope, but that is something that is outside your realm of control. What you do have control over is whether you chose each gift with the intention of pleasing and whether you choose to be grateful for someone else's gift for you.

Altered expectation: *Did I choose gifts, with love?*

༄

Yes, Lord.

༄

Then that expectation was met.

Do you choose to be appreciative of all that was given to you, and would you not prefer to choose your own kind of wallet?

ৎ

I was not being appreciative, Lord. I now choose to be.

ৎ

Example D

First expectation: I want to sit with my family and guests. Everyone enjoys the other's company.

Altered expectation: I desire that all my guests may experience warmth and love as they enter my home, enjoy a good meal, experience the moment, and be able to go home again, cognizant of the fact that they were with others who cared about them on this special day. They did not experience the day as one of loneliness.

Do you think that expectation was met, Annie?

ৎ

Yes, Lord, it appeared that way. Thank You for these insights.

ৎ

We are not quite finished, little one. You see, your son who has entered his thirtieth year still does not know My direction for him. He is uncertain of the direction that his career should take, as he does not feel that there is much future or attraction in his present field. He still has feelings for the girl he used to date some time back, but he is afraid to revisit old territory for fear of reacquaintance with heartbreak. You know that his expectation is that, since he has asked for My involvement, I will fix everything without any risk on his part. Is this a reasonable expectation, Ann? Of course it is not, so you can also stop hoping for the same!

Yes, I do read hearts, and I know you just want happiness for your son, but you also know him well enough to know that, if he doesn't have to struggle at something, he never comes to appreciate what he has actually achieved. When making difficult decisions in life, people learn to accept and appreciate ownership of their own lives. The world calls it character building. I call it soul building. Yes, Annie, this last bit of information not only applies to David but to all human beings, including you and your struggle with your weight.

It can be applied to many situations that face a person all the days of one's life from choosing to take the first step toward an encouraging parent's outstretched arms to deciding to plan one's own funeral arrangements, even if it is just writing down one's wishes on a piece of paper.

Life is, of course, about having expectations, hopes, and goals. But are these wise, challenging, and valuable expectations or self-centered, easy, and self-serving pursuits? Life is what you make it! You have a wonderful expression. If life hands you lemons, make lemonade! This may seem to be an oversimplification in some peoples' circumstances, but I assure you all that, with the combination of your lemons and My sugar, we can and will make lemonade out of each and every one of your lives, no matter how bitter it may appear.

0-0

MANY PATHS TO FINDING RELATIONSHIP WITH YOUR GOD

*D*ear Jesus, in all the years that you and I have been communicating, You so often speak of love. You seldom seem to mention our faults, sins, failings, or shortcomings except in the gentlest way. I am in the process of trying to read the journal of one of Your great creations, and I am weighed down by his preoccupation with minutiae—loss of attention during prayer, a judgmental thought, or the forgetting of a particular invocation. It causes me to question my approach to You. I have always felt relaxed with You, knowing that You love me in spite of my shortcomings. Am I too relaxed or too casual? Have I rid myself of the action sins but failed to eradicate the inaction sins or attitudinal imperfections? Lord, how can I ever come to love myself if I am forever watching for myself to slip up, convincing myself that I am blind to my faults, and constantly reminding myself of my unworthiness? Jesus, would You see a need to respond to this?

☙

Annie, write this.

GG Fortunately the Father reads hearts. He knows exactly what you are thinking and doing and the reasons why you do. He can distinguish between humility and self-righteousness, generosity of heart and duty of mind, or true love and self-love. The Father reads the motive behind all your thoughts and deeds and responds in an appropriate manner.

If a person truly wishes to grow, the Spirit will give direction and counsel. The searcher will become aware of the areas within that need attention, and that awareness will be kept in focus for them by the Spirit until the person is ready to choose to adjust the behavior and/or thinking into a more perfected behavior or thought.

You were inspired in noticing that the writings of the author of the book you were reading were going nowhere. Halfway through the book, you were finding that he was still anguishing over the same concerns. And then you saw!

You too have spent your lifetime anguishing over the fact that you have always been wrestling with your weight. You have explored this reality from every angle, looking for causes and reasons. You believe you have tried everything, and yet you still struggle.

Why? Because you believe that what you want—to be thin, to be like others, to feel good about yourself, or to lose the shame now—is more important than what you might learn from going through this experience. You cannot fathom anything better than instant thinness or the fact that I love you just the way you are. Your thoughts override Mine, and I allow this!

I do not fault you for this. I created you, and I knew full well all the implications of all the characteristics programmed into who you would have the potential to become. I also know how much perfecting each of you is capable of achieving in this lifetime, and it gives Me great joy to see you making progress.

Because the Father came to earth in the form of Jesus, He fully understands what it is like to be human and the struggle it is to perfect oneself. That is why He is so patient, understanding, and loving.

I give you life so you can grow in Spirit and relationship with Me. I give you life so you may come to experience who I am and so I may experience who you are. I give you life so We may experience who We (you and I) are. And when that occurs, My kingdom comes to earth, fully alive, fully human, and fully divine! Your perfecting leads to the furthering of My kingdom on earth.

This is why there is not just one way, one method, or one perfect formula for perfecting yourself. Each individual is an entire experience. This is why writers may appear to be giving different messages. Everyone is unique and therefore sees and hears things with his or her unique perspective. Each person will respond from his or her level of consciousness. You hear what you are ready to learn. The key to the journey is what works for you right at this moment. Search until you find what speaks to your heart and your mind.

I know all your strengths and limitations, and I will lead you to a personally designed strategy for the perfecting of your journey, which will assist in the ushering in of the kingdom. When you ask Me for help, I will make sure you do not get led astray, and you may just help someone else find his or her personal focus.

0-0

VULNERABILITY

*D*ear Jesus, I sense You suggesting that we write this morning. The pen is Yours, Lord.

☙

Annie, My Annie, write this. You have been battling an illness for the last three weeks, and now Bert has come down with what appears to be the same thing. You are worn out. You have discovered for the first time in your life just how very vulnerable you can be, vulnerability, I might add, with which the majority of the world's population is quite familiar.

You have had your eyes opened to a reality that most of the world's population lives with every day, uncertainty as to whether daily needs will be met or not. The circumstances vary, but basically it boils down to one question, "Will I be able to achieve the meeting of all my needs and responsibilities today? Will there be a safe place to sleep or have enough food or medicine, if needed? Will my home survive war, flooding, or any other catastrophe? Will there be enough money? What will happen when I am no longer able to be in control of my own circumstances?"

Annie, you felt that vulnerability for a very short period of time. Yes, I know you still have your personal concerns, but more than likely, most of them will be dealt with satisfactorily because of your background and training, where you live in the world, and your economic situation. Yes, there are those who are more financially secure than you are, but the majority of the human race does live lives of quiet desperation.

I do not speak to you like this to make you feel guilty or ashamed of what you do have. You had little control over when and where you were born or who your parents would be with the associated cultures. Many of the choices you have made though have led you to where you are at this very moment. And at present, you are in a fortunate position. You have enough money (even in retirement) to get by, but you don't have so much that you are preoccupied with the fear of losing power, position, or wealth.

Where is this communication heading?

GG I am hoping to awaken you and any others who might one day read this to the reality of your vulnerability and your subsequent reliance on Our assistance. Oddly the secure few in the world make most of the decisions for the rest, yet they have no empathy or comprehension of the needs of those for whom they make these decisions.

Banks use other peoples' money to make profits for themselves, and then as greed overwhelms them, they resort to paying less and less for the privilege of using another's money. Politicians make decisions based on the lobbying of big business rather than on the needs and concerns of those who elect them to office. Assistance is given to struggling nations based on the economic returns that might be realized by such assistance. The needs of the majority are being ignored so as to satisfy the greed of a few.

World powers have come to worship their own god, the almighty dollar. This can be compared to the building of a structure on sandy ground. There is nothing of permanent stability to hold the foundations in place should anything disturb the ground on which it is erected. As more and more decisions are based on speculation and the hunger for bigger profits grows, fewer and fewer safety features are part of the planning.

This blind pursuit of more money, greater profits, and higher numbers is just a paper walk if nothing of permanence is done with the proceeds. What are all the paints in the world to an artist if he doesn't paint a picture with them? What is the point of having great wealth when the fear of its loss overwhelms you? What's the point of having the corner on the market if too few can afford to buy what you are selling?

To understand another's vulnerability, one has to have experienced one's own vulnerability. To change the world, you must change yourself first. No amount of finger pointing and fault finding will do anything to correct the mistakes that have been made. An honest assessment of a situation—a searching out and repair of the weaknesses in any situation—is the only way to begin to regain one's control over human vulnerability.

Might I suggest a return to the basic tenet that I encouraged while I was amongst you: do unto others as you would have them do unto you. If you were all looking out for each other, not one of you would be nearly as vulnerable as you are.

By the way, until the world catches on to the above-mentioned wisdom, you can always ask Me to look after your needs. It won't all change overnight, but if you give Me a bit of time to help you make your future decisions, you may just begin to notice a difference.

0-0

DARE TO MAKE A DIFFERENCE

*A*nnie, My Annie, write this.

GG It is the I Am, the God of all peoples. I am the Creator of the universe, the Creator of all you know, the Creator of all peoples, and the Creator of you, the person who comes to read this. I have known you from before the beginning of time. I have waited for this very moment when you, for the first time, would acknowledge just how close I am to you and just how close I would like you to be to Me. Just how close am I to you?

I am your heartbeat. Feel your pulse and feel Me! When you know and love Me, our thoughts are one! You are able to see with My eyes. You are able to speak My words. You are able to transmit My love to others for Me. You and I are one!

But so few of you know this, the comprehending of the vastness of this reality. Desire the responsibility. So many of you believe what the world tells you, that you must measure up to the world's standards and that only the world's standards have any importance.

How can you maintain your status in this world if everything the world idolizes can be taken from you? So many of you strive for financial security, yet so few achieve the goal that would satisfy them. And the few who do succeed are always afraid of its loss. So many of you are preoccupied with *appearances—fitness, health, and youth—and not one of them is guaranteed or permanent for anyone. So many of you either reject or are haunted by thoughts of death, and yet it is the only guaranteed outcome for everyone. So many of you live lives that you believe others demand or want of you, never truly finding the jewels I embedded in you when I planned and formed you.*

What does it take to get you to wake up, to take the blinders from your eyes, to see truth amidst the disharmony and inequality around you? You hear the cries, and you see and feel the anger and pain, but you are paralyzed and numbed by the apparent enormity of the problem and your belief that you are too insignificant to affect a change.

I have a divine truth for you! Everything comes from Me. I Am! Before I created the world, there was nothing. This world you have come to inhabit was created by a thought, a desire, love. All is because I Am. If I Am did not exist, neither would you! You are because I chose you to be! I chose you because you have a purpose, My purpose for you!

Do you choose to know My purpose for you, or do you choose to live your life in mediocrity, making little or no impact on the evolution of mankind? Yes, you may run countries and/or control great wealth, but how does that affect the evolution of man, the stirring of humans to their ultimate greatness? You have the ability to impact the world, to make it a better place just because you exist in it. How can you do that? How can you change the world?

You cannot! But We—you and I—can! Search Me out. Start to listen when I speak to your heart, day to day, minute to minute. I am always with you to encourage, advise, comfort, and love you. Together We can change your world, and as more and more of you get the message, We will renew the face of the earth.

It is never too late. All you need is the idea, desire, and love, specifically love for yourself, others, and, ultimately, Me. Dare to make a difference!

0-0

SEXUALITY

Dear God, I sense that the topic this morning is about human sexuality, and I feel most unqualified to be dealing with this subject. For some time now, it seems You have been suggesting that our way of looking at and reacting to sex is not the healthiest. You even seem to be alluding to the possibility that our attitude toward the whole homosexual issue is archaic. As these ideas certainly are in conflict with all the old attitudes and teachings that I grew up with and because I hate to be in conflict with others, I am concerned about just how accurately I will put these ideas into words. This can be such a controversial subject, especially amongst church people, evincing gasps, disgust, shock, or at least the lowering of voices and creation of very serious facial expressions.

We seem to have a preoccupation with sexuality that unfortunately comes across most often as either crude or prudish. We have a great variety of assumed interpretations of what is meant by this or that passage from scripture, but except for "Thou shalt not commit adultery" and a reference or two about lewd conduct, not much is said about our sexuality.

This pen is Yours.

Annie, write this.

GG I have been waiting a long time for the opportunity to express My suggestions, not rules, concerning the sexuality of My finest creation, mankind. When an artist creates a masterpiece, he or she does not hide it away but shows it off, hoping that others will appreciate the skill and artistry, be it a painting, a sculpture, a symphony, a miracle cure, or a labor-saving device. When a chef creates a culinary masterpiece, he does not expect it to sit on a plate only to be admired for its eye appeal but never to be tasted.

For those of you chortling or tut-tutting about the use of these analogies, please just continue to read. Try to put aside centuries of conditioning, misunderstanding, and misinterpretation. Apart from lewd conduct (sexuality without love), the only sin that should be addressed here is that so many of you perceive sex as sin.

I created the human form. Are you suggesting that what I created is sin? I designed the penis and the vagina, each with its own unique function, and then designed how they could have further purpose when functioning together. Are you saying that I, God, created sin or there was some error in the design?

I planned that sexuality would be pleasurable for both parties. Did I, God, make a mistake? I have made it possible for a person to experience an orgasm alone, thus enabling that soul to ease built-up sexual tension without turning to rape, sexual abuse, or self-loathing, to name a few possible outcomes. Are you saying this was a mistake? I created bodies that breathe, eat, digest, urinate, defecate, and have sexual orgasms. Is it because the latter causes pleasure that you perceive it as wrong?

Do you truly believe that I, the all-loving God, would design a natural, pleasurable, involuntary function and then expect you to not use it, use it sparingly, or even abstain altogether? How cruel would that be? That would be like the parent who puts a child's favorite food in front of them but punishes them because they want it, let alone actually eat it!

It does not occur to you to give up breathing! Fortunately for you, I made that impossible. It is pretty much the same story when it comes to defecating and urinating. You would be hard-pressed to abstain from either of these functions. Doing without food for any great length of time does not serve you well either, and as many of you will attest, it is very hard to do. Is it My imagination, or is a pattern forming here? If you put a pleasure component into something, humans will find a way to distort its natural importance in life.

Yes, I created sex so I could make sure that My greatest creation would continue. I made it alluringly pleasurable so that, in spite of a predictable avoidance of responsibility on man's part, children would continue to come along. Even in this day and age when you are knowledgeable of how to avoid conception, be it artificially or through the understanding of the normal rhythms of the human body, many of you are still unable to override the excitement of the moment. I make this statement merely to highlight just how strong this (urge)ncy can be.

Once you are a living, breathing human being, sexuality is not essential for staying alive, but it is essential for being a fully alive, fully loving human, not necessarily in the acting out of the desire but in the acknowledgement and acceptance of the feelings without fear, disgust, or shame.

How many of you are comfortable with your own nakedness? Many of you have seen or read about native peoples who, until recently, have had no knowledge or contact with the modern world. Were any of them into clothing? Did they make a point of trying to cover themselves when they first met the outside world? These people are comfortable with their humanity and all that it entails. Sexuality, to them, is part of life, not something they compartmentalize, taking it out only in secret. It is just part of the natural ebb and flow of life.

Some of you may have some sense of what I am talking about if you were ever able to enjoy stripping down to the buff as a kid and skinny-dipping with your best pals. Your nakedness probably never entered your mind unless one of you cracked a joke about it. You accepted each other unconditionally.

Many of you hide behind your clothing. To truly love and to feel unconditionally loved, one has to be stripped of artifice and distrust. One of the most amazing ways of achieving this is by being able to be comfortable in your nakedness in the presence of others.

I can hear many of you rushing to form arguments of all sorts. I am not suggesting that you all walk around naked, especially in the colder climes, but believe it or not, you would soon lose your hang-ups over nakedness and sexuality if you were no longer trying to hide it.

What I really want to address here is your warped preoccupation with sex. You express shock and disgust at rape, abortion, prostitution, and the freedom with which some people move from relationship to relationship, but you seldom consider the reason for the prevalence of these things in your culture. How often does your entertainment include one or several of these activities you see as shocking and disgusting?

Mankind, to greater or lesser degrees, has pretty much become a breed of pleasure seekers, either covertly or openly. You have discovered the pleasurable side of sexuality and have chosen to discard all the rest. In doing so, you also give the uninitiated and the broken the idea that this is normal. Trust, commitment, loyalty, and unconditional love go right out the window! The deep, natural need to feel accepted for who you are is prostituted for the belief that, if someone wants to have sex with you, then you are acceptable and desirable.

You have come to use the word love indiscriminately. You say that you love another, and yet you might also be heard to say that you love to take a walk in the woods, read a book, or go shopping. The operative word here is love, but let us clarify the real meaning of the word. It should not be defined as the act of getting pleasure out of something. To truly love another or to be unconditionally loved by another can be described as "a deep, ongoing affection and respect for another in spite of their shortcomings." Sometimes a loving relationship like this may have a sexual component. That merely deepens it and sets it apart from all other relationships.

As I said before, I created sexuality to ensure the continuing population of the world, but there is so much more to it than just that. Nothing that comes from Me is one-dimensional. You are becoming more and more aware that the ability to populate the world does not depend on love. Children can be the outcome of rape, momentary excitement, arranged marriages, and now biotechnology, but none of these necessarily includes love, even though My plan will always be the best way.

So what about the other aspects of sexuality? Why did I include them if all I needed was to maintain population? If sexuality is a component of a relationship between two people who have genuine affection and respect for one another, it will deepen the intensity of that relationship. A deepened relationship will have more staying power to get people through the rough times.

Sexual feelings assist a person in defining himself or herself and can help to add color to a situation or relationship even if it is never acted upon. Sexuality provides variety and contrast to life. Sexuality can be the yeast of dreams when life appears to be unleavened.

This scribe of Mine had no desire whatsoever to tackle this subject because she, like most of you, has carried the heavy burden of sin and guilt that has been associated with sexuality for centuries. I knew that, if I continued to ask, she would eventually give Me permission to use her pen to express a truth that has needed to be brought into the divine light.

Mankind, with the help of evil (that which is not of Me), has turned sexuality into a distorted, corrupted aberration. In truth, it is one of My most beautiful gifts. This gift of physical intimacy potentiates the ability to create life, to transmit emotional wellness, to give and receive pleasure, to occasion moments of the greatest excitement, and, yet in almost the same breath, to generate wonderful release and relaxation. It is a gift to share, but you will note that several aspects may be utilized by individuals who, for whatever reason, have found themselves journeying alone.

We have only just begun to scratch the surface of this subject. We will go into it more deeply in the future, but for now, allow yourself to hear My words in your own heart. You do not have to accept carte blanche what is written here. Old, ingrained attitudes take a long time to change, especially when they have several thousand years of seniority. What I do ask is that you at least consider the possibility that maybe I did not make a mistake in the first place. Maybe I did know what I was doing.

You have changed your beliefs about many things over the years. You used to believe that, if someone got sick, it was because I was punishing him or her for some disobedience. Thank goodness that most of you have let go of that one! Or have you? You used to believe that the world was flat and the sun, moon, and stars revolved around you on a daily basis. Even more recently, as My scribe remembers well, people believed that a person could catch a cold from getting chilled. If mankind has been known to misunderstand or misinterpret certain things, is it possible that there are still other misconceptions to be righted?

Maybe the only change that needs to take place is one of awareness— awareness of the bigger picture, the larger dimension, the greater benefit to the individual and all of humanity—when the gift of sexuality ceases to be used in the absence of love.

I ask you to think this through for yourself. Do not slam the door of your mind, for I am asking all of mankind to grow in My wisdom and love.

0-0

HOMOSEXUALITY

*D*ear Jesus, several things have caused the topic of homosexuality to be loitering in my mind. One of those things is a news item about a school banning a student from bringing a same-sex partner to the dance. I know what I have been taught and what the current attitude seems to be in the Western world, but something inside my head suggests that we are not looking at this whole issue with wisdom or true understanding. Do You care to respond, Lord?

☙

Annie, write this.

GG There are many people in the world whose sexuality does not conform to what much of society considers normal. What is normal?

When I first created mankind, sexuality was as natural as eating, sleeping, or relieving oneself. There was no shame attached to the viewing or handling of parts of the body associated with sexuality. It just was!

In present day, many of you as children probably remember being most interested in the naked body if you grew up in a home where modesty made sure that you never saw parents without an appropriate covering. Sometimes a sibling or friend solved the mystery for you. Quite often that modesty caused sexuality to become something that one only whispered about. And because you now believed that you could not ask questions, sexuality started to hold an interest for you at a much younger age. You know that an interest in sexual activity in the uninitiated is generated from within by the natural maturation of the human body and the glandular production of hormones. I, the Creator, designed and created you all to experience this. I doubt that many of you would say that I made a mistake.

As the human enters puberty and continues to grow, so does the interest in sexuality. Exactly when that interest emerges might depend on how soon the adolescent becomes aware of modern-day advertising, publications, adult movies, TV and videos, or something a friend might say or do. (Sexual abuse is another whole issue.) The Western world has a preoccupation with sexuality, so it is not surprising that interest in it begins at quite a young age.

Sexuality in nature occurs without premeditation. It occurs naturally in a regular pattern, depending on the particular species in question. There is no thought involved, merely a knowing that it is time and an innate knowing of how to proceed with an appropriate mate.

Note that I said an appropriate mate. What is an appropriate mate? Up until recently, this scribe believed, as many of you still do, that there is something wrong with being homosexual. Lately some have even gone so far as to call it intrinsically evil.

One evening, a group of her spiritual friends was meeting, and during that gathering, one of the gentlemen shared a bit of his journey. He was a married man with children. One son was homosexual. He shared how the situation had long been most distressing for him and his wife.

Within the last year, he had lost his wife to illness, and his grief, sense of loss, sadness, and confusion were still very fresh to him when his overwhelmed son came to him to tell him that his companion had just died of AIDS. He took one look at the obvious agony on his son's face and knew beyond a shadow of a doubt that they were both experiencing the same emotions. He could see and feel that his son's relationship had truly been a loving one. His son's suffering was just as acute as his own. This gentleman went on to share with the group that evening that this awareness had both shocked him and permanently changed his perception of homosexual relationships.

His story also changed this scribe's perception of the homosexual state, especially when it has become evident that homosexuality is not something that a person chooses. Considering the hell that many are made to experience at the hands of others due to this persuasion, who in his or her right mind would choose it? It becomes a characteristic, just like height, gender, hair color, or nationality. It is an inborn instinct that I allow. Did I make a mistake?

O-O

DEALING WITH ANXIETY

Where do I begin, Lord? You seem to be telling me to write in this book this morning even though I would prefer to use my personal journal. This feels like private stuff, not something that a reader would be interested in or benefit from.

ॐ

Trust Me!

ॐ

Last evening two friends came over for prayer. One told me that the other had an image of me in a cage during a period in his meditation time. I was first amazed that I had been a part of his prayer time and, second, I had been perceived as in a cage. That is exactly how I have been feeling for the last several months.

Since Bert retired, he is home most of the time. My prayer and work routine is gone. I can remember writing some time ago that the family was not to derail me from my writing, but as dates in this book and my journal attest, I have not been following that directive.

Our son moved home in January, and his frustration over what he is to do with his life rubs off on me. He does not wish to be a dental technician the rest of his life, but at this point, he is doing the work, saving his money, and keeping his eyes and ears open for insight. It weighs on us to see him adrift without direction.

We had a frenzy of activity all winter and spring, or at least Bert did. He was completing a correspondence course as well as being the only catechist for six candidates in our church instructional group. He also completed all sorts of refurbishing to the house before friends from Holland came for a three-week visit.

Two or three days into that visit, his anxiety returned with a vengeance, and for the last month, he has experienced moderate panic attacks and anxiety nearly daily. A trip to the doctor obtained a mild relaxant, but old terrors seemed to haunt him. He has finally agreed to see a counselor, but the anticipation has made yesterday and last night very anxious, to say the least. This would normally be a day that I would be babysitting our grandson, but it is probably wiser for me to go with Bert this first time. So I called our daughter to ask if she could delay his arrival until after our appointment. She was in tears and could not talk.

Lord, my anxiety is surfacing a little here, and I'm overeating again. My clothes are tight, and that caged person needs some of Your hands-on wisdom. With two deaths and several friends being diagnosed with cancer, it feels tense these days. Maybe that has been the reason for the back pain and frequent headaches. Jesus, do You wish to respond?

CR

When have I ever not responded, Annie?

Annie, write this.

GG I have asked you to include this concern in this manuscript because everyone, at one time or another in one's life, experiences periods of high stress. You are right! The reader will not be as interested in what you are stressed about as in the fact that you are stressed. That is the common denominator, the stressful experience.

Each person has his or her own areas of weakness, the particular circumstances that, when present, can tax their composure to the limit. Bert, Karen, and David are all experiencing varying degrees of stress at this moment in time but for different reasons. You, oh mother hen, are doing just as you have always done, worrying in silence, never sharing your own anxieties about them and yourself with anyone. You think that everyone else has his or her own concerns, and in comparison to others, "My worries must seem insignificant."

Ann, as I said earlier, everyone has unique weakness. When certain circumstances occur, it makes them susceptible to self-doubt and thus fear. Yes, self-doubt incubates fear. Constant self-doubt breeds anxiety and panic. But anxiety also has a positive side. It forces action, and in your case, it has forced you to do something that you have been putting off, writing, even though you know and remember My directive to not let family concerns derail your job as My scribe.

Anxiety has also forced Bert to agree to see this counselor this morning even though last night was most unbearable (not an accurate description as you did both get through it). I would like you to report here how the day pans out and compare it to the degree of dread that accompanied its arrival. We will continue this correspondence in a few hours. I love you all, and remember to trust Me!

Well, what did I say? Was it as bad as you had expected? Did Sam not confirm all you have been telling Bert over these years and especially these last few weeks? You had been observing him and listening to his fears lately while beginning to doubt your own wisdom and wondering, "What if—"

Then you get home and are ready to face the next crisis, which was Karen's, only to hear in her voice that the worst was over and the day had worked out better for her because she had stayed home. Imagine!

Also don't forget the "no place to park" just as you drove up to Sam's building this morning. As you were trying to decide where you might find an available parking spot, a car parked immediately ahead of you pulled out, and you were able to pull right in. Am I good, or am I good?

ଓ

Thank You, Lord!

ଓ

You're welcome, but now We're not quite finished. This has eased the moment for you, but what about our readers who are about to say, "Well, that's all fine and dandy for them, but what about my anxiety?"

For the readers, each of you, remember that anxiety is overload—too much of one thing or a lot of lesser things that never seem to get resolved in a manner that satisfies you. What you think would satisfy you may or may not be appropriate, but the issue remains. You are experiencing overload.

The overload stems from a feeling of an inability to control, fix, or perform. It can relate to one or many aspects of your life: your job, your appearance, your friendships, your sociability, and so on. The older you are and the longer you have carried this disbelief about yourself, the more areas of your life may be connected to or affected by anxiety.

This scribe and her husband have only just begun to do the work of untangling truth from fiction regarding how they perceive themselves or how they have come to believe that others see them. There is work ahead for them, but they have asked Me for answers, and this is the next step for them. Bert has coped with his anxiety for close to forty years. Ann had a taste of it for three or four years so she could be a little more understanding, but both journeys have been directed by Me, as will your journey, if you will allow Me to accompany you.

Anxiety is not a mental illness. It is a response to overload. Each of your circumstances is unique, as are your journeys, so it stands to reason that each approach would be uniquely designed for your individual needs. Give Me permission to guide you toward healing, and be willing to become willing to do the work needed to achieve that healing. And there will be no limitations on what you might expect from your life on earth.

Not one of you is waste! Each of you has a divine purpose, and no one is asked to go it alone without My intimate attention and love. I am able to work with anything to achieve the eventual arrival of My kingdom on earth, even anxiety!

0-0

YOU HAVE MY PERMISSION TO ASK QUESTIONS

*F*ather God, we here in our region have just experienced the World Youth Day activities—the preparation, the buildup, the arrival, and the aftermath. For reasons that are not altogether clear, I was not the slightest bit interested. It is only now, after all is over and done and I hear raves from the people who were involved, that I question my disinterest, even irritation. Maybe I should have asked this question sooner so I too might have been more supportive.

☙

First Ann, we will give you some insight into this disinterest. Your youth was one of limitations, getting by, not fitting in, standing on the sidelines, not being chosen. Your initial reaction to this whole endeavor zeroed in on all the millions of young people who could not be here, who would stand in the sidelines, able only to watch as others participated. You felt that those who would be coming were the advantaged, and you felt resentment that you were being asked to give financial and emotional support to these advantaged at a time when your own finances and emotions were being seriously tested.

You also did not experience any inner call to be involved. You did not sense that I was asking you to participate, and in essence, you did support your own church's involvement by listening to all the speeches, not verbalizing your objections, and participating in all the fund-raisers. You did what you felt moved to do.

But you are more interested in what We thought of your reactions and God's perspective of the whole undertaking. Ann, you are reluctant to write anything here because you watched very little of the proceedings on television, and all else might be based on what others have told you. You feel that your bias is going to color what you are about to write down. How could you, who you feel to be quite insignificant, dare to write what you fear may be a somewhat critical response when the Catholic church and its leader and hierarchy supported this effort?

GG Ann, write this. Many positive memories will have been created for those who did participate, and I am pleased with all who willingly participated in the proceedings. If the experience goes on to deeply impact the minds, hearts, and souls of the participants, then we have achieved the ultimate goal, to bring people into or closer to the kingdom. And by that, we mean giving them a deeper relationship with their God, their neighbor, and themselves. Does it take all this time, effort, and money to achieve this goal, or might there be less costly, yet more far-reaching ways, to accomplish the same outcome?

Only those who participated will truly be able to say whether it sincerely affected their personal approach to life, and that may take some years before a true evaluation might be realized. If those who were able to attend went home to share their experiences and worked to improve the lot of those left behind, then we have progress.

The message of My love for each and every human being who walks the face of the earth is a message for all, not just a select few. No one is excluded. Did the pilgrimage send out this message? Did the multitude hear My voice? Did the words speak to all who might have heard? Ultimately, what were the objectives of the organizers, and what will be the overall outcome? Only time will produce the answers.

I am everywhere. You can meet Me in a huge crowd, in solitude, in the middle of a storm, or in the silence of fog. My message is simply love. Desire to love Me, all mankind, and yourself, and I will assist you in doing so. It is not significant where and when you begin to learn these lessons, but only that you do!

0-0

THE UNFOLDING OF TRUTH

Lord, for quite a while now, I have felt that You have been leading me to explore the bigger picture. You have caused me to look at many of the attitudes and beliefs I grew up with and to explore the validity of my perceptions. You have caused me to reconsider the authority of the church to which I give my support. You have led me to explore more deeply my understanding of Your love for us, and in doing so, I have had to reconsider how I perceive evil, sin, salvation, and love of neighbor and self.

All this unsettling exploration has also caused a new awareness of what it means to love You—the ever-present, all-powerful, all-knowing God who, because of Your great love for us, chose to come to earth Yourself in the form of a man so we could better relate to You and have some sense of who and what You are.

Many of the insights that I believe You have shared with me are not so easily shared with others. Many persons can and quite often do get upset if they perceive that their religion and/or faith (depending on the depth of their spirituality) is being brought into question. What is the point of my journey of awakening if it is to be perceived as the work of the devil, New Age, or the musings of a non-academic, unemployed, middle-aged grandmother who thinks that she hears God? How preposterous! How arrogant!

☙

Annie, write this.

GG When I first introduced Myself to you so many years ago, you had no doubt about who was speaking to you. You knew it certainly was not you or your ideas. (Others who knew you and had read some of our communication confirmed this). They, as well as you, felt an immense peace flowing out from the words I had you write down.

Now after so many miles together, you have become more assimilated with Me and more accustomed to My continuing Presence. And you find it harder to distinguish that which is you and that which is Me. The worldly you is stepping aside and allowing Me more and more space in which to reside, but as yet, you have not totally died to self. Part of you still fears what others will think and say.

When you no longer fear the opinions of others, you will be truly ready to bring some of My more healing and life-giving ideas and concepts to a very needy world. When you consider how slowly this manuscript is being assembled, we may have succeeded in doing just that by the time you put the last of these communications into print.

As I proofread the previous sentence, I start to smile. It has been more than fifteen years since I initially started this manuscript. I ask, "Am I ready now, Lord?"

In 1 Corinthians 13, a passage says, "When I was a child, I used to talk as a child, think like a child and reason like a child. When I became a man (woman), I put childish ways aside." Annie, it is time for mankind to put childish ways aside. It is time to grow and begin to reason, not as a worldly person reasons but as offspring of Mine would reason.

GOD GLASSES

Children are taught rules, for the most part, to keep them safe and out of trouble and for their own personal health and welfare. As they mature, they begin to understand the reasons for the rules and are then hopefully able to decide for themselves if this or that rule is still a valid guideline. Being in bed by nine o'clock is a suitable rule for a five-year-old (and more than likely for his parents), but it becomes no longer appropriate as the child gets older.

As mankind matures, it begins to understand more and more of the truth that defines reality. What used to be considered a truth can change overnight, as in the case of the belief that the world was flat, the sun revolved around the Earth, or witches should be killed.

When you consider how much has been hidden or unknown to man in a worldly sense, does it not seem reasonable that spirituality, which is unseen, might also have a vastness of comprehension still to be discovered? If this is the case (and I assure you that it is), then how am I going to get this information across to you? It is often when one or two people get an idea in their head and start to explore its parameters, inside and outside the box, that new and monumental discoveries are made. Hence you have flight, medicines, the radio, the microscope, and so forth.

I have been inspiring persons since their appearance on earth. I spoke to Abram alone, not his whole family. I spoke to Moses alone. I revealed Myself to him in the desert. When I gave him the first bits of God wisdom, the Ten Commandments, for my children, I didn't call a great number of Israelites up to a conference table on top of Mount Sinai. I called one man aside who was familiar with My voice, and I gave him My communication. I continue to do this today.

When I speak, My words say, "Let those who have ears, listen." In all things, I give you free choice. Everyone is responsible for how he or she reacts to the lives presented to them, the opportunities, the challenges, the hardships, the relationships, the faith experiences, and, ultimately, their personal salvation. I offer these things to you freely. You choose to accept or reject them or to act or just react.

It is the same for Our communications, Annie. People will have the opportunity to read or hear about what We say to you and a handful of other listeners (those who have ears) and decide for themselves whether they wish to accept or reject a maturing perception of Me. It is faith development, and like everything I have ever created, there will always be something more to discover. Just when you think that you have finally figured it all out, I allow the blinders to be removed from your eyes, and with the help of God glasses, you are given the opportunity to grow and see more clearly.

I love you all.

0-0

DARE TO RISK FINDING TRUTH

*D*ear Jesus, the previous writings on sexuality and homosexuality may not seem congruent with religious teaching and, in many cases, even the world's. At this point, while these words are not in print, I can just keep silent, but it does cause me to question my discernment when the whole world or a mighty large portion of it probably would object vehemently. I am not a risk taker, Lord; nor am I particularly courageous.

༄

Annie, write this.

GG There is very little in life that remains the same, whether it is in a single lifetime or in the passing centuries. Even that which I originally created millions of years ago has evolved slowly with the passing of time. You humans are evolving at a faster pace because you have been gifted (yes, I said gifted) with free will that introduces options and choices into your daily existence and your eventual evolution. These options and choices were permitted to assist you to learn from your errors—to grow, change, mature, and perfect. If I had not given you free choice, your love for Me would have been programmed into your souls. I wanted My children to love Me because they felt love for Me, not because they didn't know how to do anything else. I did not wish to create robots.

I created each of you so you not only experience the pleasure of life in the hereafter but also in My kingdom here on earth. That is what life, as you know it, is all about, the eventual arrival of My kingdom here on earth. Until that moment arrives, you will discover that there are two aspects to yourself. There is the self that you believe yourself to be, the ego-controlled self. And then there is the spiritual self, or true self, which recognizes the God within. In both forms, you make choices. As mankind grows in knowledge, understanding, and wisdom (which might be defined as God's insight), he or she becomes more and more able to reflect Me and who and what I am.

But evolution is a slow process. For every three steps forward in universal understanding, there are inevitably one or two steps backward, for mankind has a tendency of seeing Me as a judgmental, punishing God. You have been afraid to test the waters of spirituality, believing that, if you go too far, you will incur My wrath. I promise you that, if you are truly seeking My truth, I will always guide you back, should you get lost.

If I were the kind of God that many of you believe Me to be, I would not blame you for steering clear or being afraid of Me. If a child is just learning to ride a bicycle, he or she is quite likely to fall and scrape themselves a few times. If the child expected or feared criticism for falling during this time, the child might attempt to practice secretly or never even make the effort to try. Is that the kind of parent you believe Me to be?

I can hear several of you coming up with all sorts of "Yes buts," but the analogy is still applicable. Man may come up with a new idea or concept, only to find out painfully that he or she has got it wrong, but if none of you attempt to explore new ways of looking at old ideas, faith and spirituality will not remain vibrant. That is one of the reasons that you find more and more people shopping around for something that feeds their souls. Doing exactly the same thing week after week, month after month, and year after year without any variation causes boredom and loss of interest. There is so much still to learn about Who I am, but there is also so much I want you to experience about who **you are** and all the potential I packed into each and every one of you!

I do not want you walking through this life that I have given you focused only on finding a formula of behavior that you believe will guarantee that you will not burn in hell for the rest of eternity. I want you to enjoy this experience and to be passionate about it, looking forward to the excitement of the unfolding adventure.

I gave you free will so you could and would make choices. I did not do this to create the yardstick that I might use to decide your inevitable fate, but to give you opportunities that would cause you to have to dig deeply within yourselves so as to discover the incredible strengths and talents that lie waiting to be discovered. Free will means just that! You are free to make choices.

When this scribe's son was about four years old, she knew that, if she put some broccoli and a piece of chocolate cake in front of him and asked him to make a choice, he'd choose the cake. He was free to make a choice. He would not have made that choice based on which one was better for him. He's still not terribly fond of broccoli, but now that he's an adult, he may just as likely ask for a piece of fruit in lieu of cake. He has matured and learned more about food, and he now has the knowledge to make wiser decisions. It is the same with the spiritual journey. As you grow in understanding and love of Me, you make choices that you want to make based on what you know your inner needs to be.

I would like you all to see the bigger picture that will take you beyond ritual, tradition, habit, and what others have told you that I demand of you. I would like you all to wake up and to come alive, to explore your individual potential that is discovered and released when you are in relationship with Me, when you and Jesus become friends. Yes, I did say "friends!"

Annie, you have been on this journey for a while now. You have come to know that I love you unconditionally. You know now that, even if you might have misinterpreted My words on sexuality (and you have not), I would not condemn you because you are truly searching out My truth. Your greatest concern is what others will think of you if you seem to them to be suggesting that there is another way to look at sexuality, a more open or healthier approach, a focus as seen through the eyes of God.

Annie, I am asking you to be My scribe, to write down to the best of your ability the ideas that I present to you. I am asking you because you are a good listener who has not been educated by theological standards, and you genuinely desire to assist in the furthering of My kingdom here on earth.

Seeing the bigger picture enables you to begin to think outside the box. I am infinite. You will never fully comprehend what that means until We are reunited in Spirit, but if you open yourself up to all I am willing to impart, you will begin to be able to perceive the multidimensional characteristics of a life lived in and through the Spirit.

All you need do is ask for My guidance and go forth. Yes, you will make mistakes. Yes, you might get hurt. Yes, you may take a wrong turn, making what appears to be a mistake, but the alternative, the safer approach, merely leads to indifference, boredom, and mediocrity. It is time now for mankind to collectively discover its true potential, its ability to reflect the true nature of its Creator.

Because of Me, you have the potential to work miracles, to heal yourselves and others, to enlighten, to enable, to prevent, to protect, to move from one location to another, to know, to hear, to see, and, most importantly, to love. I would like My kingdom to flourish right here on earth, but that cannot happen until you reflect Me to one another. When that happens, you will discover Me in your midst.

Please do not be afraid of Me! I love you all unconditionally, and I do not punish. You are merely unable to relate to Who you think I am or who you have been led to believe that I am. Yes, you will suffer the consequences of lives lived, driven by anger, hatred, greed, jealousy, arrogance, and intolerance. You have all been given free choice to make your own decisions, but asking for a bit of guidance before you make a decision may reduce some of those consequences.

Come, dare to look at the bigger picture. Dare to risk finding truth. I promise you that you will never regret your decision, and the world will be a better place because you did!

0-0

MOMENTARY THOUGHTS AND FEEDBACK

Dear God, You say that I am to put myself down on these pages. The other day a spiritual friend expressed this same idea to me, and later You reminded me of the same directive as I was editing an older manuscript.

This morning, was it You who urged Bert to read to me out of a book that has been sitting around here unopened for quite a while on being a prophet? Something inside me resonated with what he was reading, *Wildmen, Warriors and Kings* by Patrick Arnold S. J. Is this not, in essence, arrogance on my part to consider thinking of myself as a prophet?

ೞ

Annie, did you decide to be a writer?

ೞ

No, Lord, definitely not!

ೞ

Even if you had, would you have chosen a format in which God was actually speaking to you?

※

Absolutely not! I never thought that You would speak to ordinary people, saints maybe, but not us average, everyday type of beings.

※

Do we really need to pursue this particular bit of dialogue?

※

Okay, I hear you.

※

Good. Next concern?

※

Where do You want me to go from here?

※

I want you to continue just as usual, in dialogue. I have much to impart, and you will have many questions as time moves on. I look forward to this more intimate format. I wish for us to show others how useful I can be to them in their own personal journeys and for you all collectively.

Let's have a cup of coffee!

0-0

USING GOD

Dear God, You are telling me to write it like it is. I am experiencing great swings of emotion. One minute I feel okay about myself. And then the bottom falls out, and I hate my size and my uncertainty of who I am. Am I a reasonably smart, worthwhile human being or merely a person who only thinks she is? To the world, I am someone who has stayed home all my life. After having my first child, I never had a paying job again. With no income and no potential, I am a waste of space. And the more I eat, the bigger waste of space I become. Lord, what in heaven is wrong with me? Why can I not sustain abstinence from eating more than I need? I have been asking You this for years! I have prayed again and again to change, but when push comes to shove, I override the "don't eat that" with "I'll just have a little or just one piece" or "I'll start the diet again tomorrow." I hate the way this kind of behavior makes me feel, and look! I need serious help!

಄

Do you?

಄

I think I do, and if I don't, why do I feel so down? Tonight I just want to crawl into bed and have the world go away.

☙

So why are you writing?

☙

I guess I keep hoping that there is some piece of information that I have been overlooking or that I still have to learn. I keep hoping that, at some point, I'm going to hit upon this one bit of understanding, and then this body will have no difficulty becoming slimmer and staying that way. Tonight I feel so hopeless, Lord! I've been told that hopeless is a word in the definition of a stronghold. How do I overcome a stronghold, Papa?

☙

With Our help, little one. You cannot do it alone. You keep forgetting. You ask for the help and then expect to be able to do it alone.

☙

Okay, how do You go about helping me?

☙

By giving you the strength to endure, to override the food thoughts, and to do the growth work necessary to achieve your goal. Annie, how would our relationship grow if you did not need My help? I want a relationship with all My children, and seeing as how you cannot see Me, there has to be something that causes you to search Me out.

O-O

☙

Can we try again, Lord?

ଔ

Yes, of course! Absolutely!

ଔ

I am asking for Your help, starting right now.

USING GOD (CONTINUED)

*D*ear God, I'm feeling old and frail. Most of the time, I feel that life is passing me by. I believe I am feeling sorry for myself. I'm struggling with what to write, even if it should be in this book. I guess I can always tear out the pages, if need be.

ॐ

Annie, I hear you. You are ashamed of yourself. You are thinking that you know Me so well. How can you feel so down in the dumps? Maybe you have some legitimate reasons for feeling abandoned yet again. You are thinking that other people have much more pressing matters than you have to cope with so you should be feeling thankful that life is as simple as it is.

Annie, I want you to work through these feelings that you are having. Others have to know how to do this, and these down feelings are an ideal example of how to do just that. Dump on Me, and let Me give you some input.

ॐ

Okay, the most present thought right now is this back of mine. I pinched the nerve just a few days ago. The pain has eased, but it still twinges. I was cutting a few late-season hydrangeas a few minutes ago, and I've pinched it again. I'm only fifty-seven, Lord!

What will I be like next year, in five years, and so forth? How will I cope when I'm old? I tried the gym. That, I think, is where all this continuous pain started. Do I just go back to walking and some gentler back exercises?

☙

Annie, isn't it amazing how you have many of the answers already in your possession! How would it be if you tried that for a week or two? Let's make an assessment then!

0-0

KNOWING AND APPRECIATING ONESELF

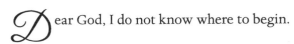ear God, I do not know where to begin.

ତଃ

Begin with the pain of yesterday.

ତଃ

I'm driving home alone, trying to control the tears so I'm able to see the road, a road I have never been on before, both literally and emotionally. I have just dropped off Bert and his friend Lawry at the start of a bicycle path that will take two days to traverse. This, like the camping trips to Algonquin Park, is another step in Bert's progress to overcome the inner fear that he has had to deal with all his life. Possibly one comes by this naturally if one is born in The Hague in 1942 as the bombs are dropping while your mother is birthing you but she is not sure that any of the family will survive the next couple minutes, let alone the next hour, week, month, or year! Strangely, in spite of the fact that he's making great progress and I am thrilled for him, I feel abandoned.

Emotions are breaking over me, engulfing me in what I believe to be self-pitying thoughts. Great! Off Bert goes to experience the exhilaration of another life challenge (and I know I am thrilled for him as no one should have to live in fear for over forty years), but I feel worn out, used up, and abandoned!

I have not had a paying job since we had our children because it was always more convenient for me to be available should Bert's anxiety become overwhelming for him. I filled my days with volunteer work, which was more accommodating to sudden changes of availability, and that used to occur from time to time. How often things were planned, only to have them fall through because of his anxiety. How often I would put my own feelings away in a drawer so I could help Bert deal with his issues.

As I watch him grow, mature, study, do these exciting things that I believe I could never do (maybe I don't even want to), give incredibly skilled talks, and get articles published in various papers and magazines, I find myself falling in love with him all over again. I find myself wondering, if now that he no longer needs me, will he discover that he never really loved me? Do I even know what love feels like or how to love?

Okay, God, I think that about sums it up, the pain and the fog. Where do I go from here?

☙

When you were so gloomy the evening prior to the trip, Bert asked if you were feeling okay. With intense effort not to appear as if you were feeling sorry for yourself, you stated that you felt as though your life was a waste of space. His "Oh, come on!" type of comment made you walk away. Presently, he responded, "Ann, if it weren't for you, where would I be?" I allowed you to hear this comment in your heart, but the timing was off. It was time for bed.

The next morning you wanted to be supportive of this new cycling adventure, but you could not shed the emotional pain in your chest. You wanted to appear to be your usual 'up' self in front of Lawry, but your thoughts were overwhelming you. You wanted to smile and wave them off, but you quickly got into the car and left so neither of them would see your face and tears. You also noted that Bert did not wave good-bye as you took off. And you felt guilty. Why? You knew he was probably somewhat anxious, but you were more interested in your own self-pitying thoughts.

Now we are up to where you were driving down the unfamiliar road with the deluge of tears cascading down your cheeks, under your chin, and down your neck. Good thing you were wearing a turtleneck! What did you do then?

꩜

I needed to stop the thoughts that kept overwhelming me, to calm down, to ease the pain in my chest. (Or was I having a heart attack?) I started a rosary. I knew that You and Mary cared about me, but my thoughts were making me so tense and anxious. I was not coping as I should!

Then You reminded me of Bert's comment the night before, "Ann, where would I be without you?" I started to think about that, and some of the darkness lifted. If the living of my life, in all its limitations, was beneficial to the development of whom Bert was becoming today, then maybe my life, as I have lived it, has not been a waste of space. You, the Christ, lived Your life for our advancement (life to the fullest), so maybe a non-exciting end is worth the outcome if someone else accomplishes Your plan for him because I existed.

꩜

Okay, hold it for a moment. I want you to redirect your thoughts. In your inimitable way, you are still giving this situation a negative connotation, one of being used. How do you feel about seeing it as a building block in My plan? Does that change your perspective?

☙

Yes, Lord, it actually does. I would like to believe that You still have some enjoyable, maybe even exciting or exhilarating, work for me to do. Maybe it just has not surfaced yet. I've not been successful with any of the other books that have so far been put into print. Finances certainly seem to cause me concern. Lord, I ask for that inner strength to persevere.

☙

Annie, I thank you for writing all this down on paper. Your feelings were/are not self-pitying. You think that they are because you were reduced to tears, but tears can also be very useful in diluting tension. You believe that, if you are coping (without any tears), then you are doing it correctly. But I do not ask you to just cope. I also want you to learn about yourself and grow. You are already a wonderful, vital human being with much still to experience and share. As a counselor said, "Now it's your turn to grow, to heal, to experience life to the full." Stay close and connected. We will get you out into the sunshine again.

0-0

REGARDING THE DEATH OF A LOVED ONE

*D*ear God, I was talking to a friend yesterday whose husband passed away this last summer. She was telling me how she wished that she could convince her adult children that their father was not far off somewhere but rather quite close, approachable, and still most interested in helping them just the way he would have when he was alive. She herself is certainly experiencing grief, but she does not feel abandoned, just separated. She hurts for her children, all six of them, who are having a hard time accepting their father's death and missing him deeply. Lord, I told her that I would approach You on this matter. Do You wish to respond to this concern at this time?

ೆ

Annie, write this.

GG To all who are experiencing the loss of someone you love, note that I addressed this to those of you who are grieving for someone you love. Yes, I intentionally used the present tense, for the spirit of the person you are missing is very much alive and still quite able to experience your love for him or her and his or her love for you.

They are not dead and gone in the sense that is so often humans' understanding. They have returned to their original dimension, that of spirit, which is your natural state and the one that most closely resembles Me. In this state, you are perfect. My wisdom, My understanding, My compassion, and My love, all that I am is now visible in the person that you understand to be dead. You also possibly see yourself as alone and abandoned by them. Not so!

Man's natural state is that of spirit. Each and every one of you humans is presently in a very temporary state. Before you were born into humanity, you lived a perfect existence, which is the creation and extension of Me. You exist in that state before you are born, and you return to that state after you have completed your assignment on earth.

All your God-given characteristics, all the unique gifts of which you can avail yourself, and all you become in your lifetime due to the combination and utilization of these things, continue to define your spirit after you die (resume your original form).

In spirit form, you return to the Oneness of all life, which means you are constantly tuned in to all life, that which is in spirit form and that which is in human form. Because of this, you are perpetually present to all that lives, which implies you are forever present to all souls, regardless of their state. You who are living are forever surrounded by the souls of all or the Oneness. We are all one. I, the Creator, created life in all forms, and you are an integral part of that creation.

So, in essence, the person whose physical absence is causing you such sadness is closer to you in their present state than they ever were able to be in human form. They know your thoughts as you think them. They know your pain and your joy. If you take the time to become more cognizant of your spirit form, which is an integral part of you even as a living, breathing human being, then you will be able to return to communion with the soul you are missing. There you will discover the love and comfort, which will assist the human side of you to accept this temporary separation. There also you will find Me and all I offer to any one of My creations as they walk through their human journey.

Come quiet yourself. And immerse yourself in the healing quality of communion with the Oneness.

I am 0-0.

A MESSAGE ON CHRISTMAS EVE

Dear Jesus, we are supposedly celebrating Your birth tomorrow, but it is frequently hard to reflect on the awe and wonder of the reality of what You did for us amidst all the busyness and noise that we have allowed Christmas to become.

I guess what I'm yearning for are feelings brought about by silence, holiness, gently falling snow, hymns, dimmed lights, and candles or maybe the old excitement that went with having small children around who were anticipating the imminent arrival of Santa Claus.

We seem to have lost sight of the reason for the season, Lord. Would You be willing to help us in refocusing, getting our priorities straightened out, or maybe even giving us a new way of looking at this celebration instead of bemoaning the fact that too much has changed to ever recapture the past?

Lord God, what would You say to this materialistic and somewhat jaded generation, many of whom rarely think of You and then only when we are desperate? Lord God, what do You say to us who do try hard to give You our attention, only to be derailed by life and all its distractions? Lord God, what do You say to us who find this time of year so hard emotionally for whatever reason?

This pen is awaiting Your Christmas message, Lord.

☙

GG Let those who read this hear these words with the ears of their hearts! I come bearing good tidings. Yes, even tonight, all these years later, I bring you all good tidings for unto you a child was born. A Savior was given. That child was born into the human race to assure you that I, the God of this universe, love you all.

I poured myself into that human form, living a very modest lifestyle for most of those thirty-three years until it was time to accomplish My true purpose. Christ walked the face of this earth so you would know that I understand just how difficult life can be. As it has been said, "If you know Christ, you know Me!"

My arrival on earth was the greatest gift that the human race has ever received. In spite of what you may believe, I had no more power than is naturally available to each and every one of you, if only you were aware of your natural inheritance as children of God and if you trusted your ability to utilize it.

You have heard the statement, "This and more you shall do!" These are not idle, empty words. This is fact. Truth!

If you are aware of My story, you know I was able to walk on water, subject the weather to My wishes, heal the sick, raise the dead, cast out demons, change water into another substance, and read peoples' hearts and minds, and I still say to you, "This and more you shall do!"

I am the source of this power, and you, like Me, are the natural recipients of these gifts if you would but ask and believe. Does this seem somewhat far-fetched (exaggerated) make-believe?

To begin with, it will. At this point in your spiritual development, you are far removed from this reality, this truth. You are infants, just as I was, powerless. But faith, spirituality, and relationship with your Father Creator is developmental. Just as a child grows physically, so are faith and spirituality supposed to be part of the dynamic growth process. Relationship with your Creator God is meant to be a vital, intimate relationship, an ever-deepening communion between God and man.

You are being invited to become familiar with what is your natural inheritance, the power of the Holy Spirit, which was My parting gift to you all as I returned to the Father. To learn more, you must draw closer to us, the Trinity (Father, Son, and Holy Spirit). Your reason for learning must come from an honest desire to improve the well-being of all your brothers and sisters. The desire for self-edification will blind you to the truths that must be utilized to comprehend these gifts.

Once you begin to make manifest the power of the Holy Spirit, it will become your top priority to acknowledge and proclaim from whence the power comes. Humility will be the garment of the heart of all who will become skilled practitioners. You will become fishers of men, shepherds to My most precious flock, all of mankind. I will be your teacher. You will become My healers, and together We will renew the face of the earth.

As the world prepares to celebrate My birth in its own particular way, I ask You to consider this invitation to receive My greatest gift to you, the power of the Holy Spirit. All you need is desire; willingness to love your God, your neighbor, and yourself; and willingness to find the time to spend in dialogue with Me as I teach you all you will need to know.

May the reading of this communication be the first of the many gifts that you will begin to receive, and may the coming years be the most joy-filled and productive of your lifetime.

0-0

A NEW YEAR'S MESSAGE

*D*ear God, I do not know what to actually write here. It's 5:30 a.m. I cannot sleep, and I feel weird. I'm shaking and cannot seem to stop. We went out to dinner at some friends' house last evening and saw the New Year in with them and two other couples. We ate and then played cards. I had a glass of wine with dinner.

I'm wide awake and have no idea what is going on in this body of mine. Anxiety, heart attack, flu, or indigestion? I've run the gamut of diagnoses in my head using the limited knowledge that I possess. Even though I feel weird, I'm not scared, I'm not in pain, and I'm able to think clearly. What's going on, Lord? Are You allowing this just so I will pick up the pen? Am I even able to hear You?

ଔ

Annie, you are indeed!

GG Yes, I most assuredly am allowing this strange feeling. You have not been able to write with the house being filled with people pretty much all of the time. When I arranged a quiet time yesterday afternoon, you opted to do other things. This would not have been necessary had I been able to communicate with you then.

"What do I have to say that is so urgent?" you ask.

Annie, I need you to have some time with Me when you are unlikely to be distracted by others. We need time alone for what I want to relate to you and all others who will come to read this in the future. I, the Creator of the universe and Father to all of mankind, have a common message for everyone who walks the face of this earth. As you prepare to experience another year, I make a suggestion, a reminder.

Strive to live your lives in love. Strive to love Me, your neighbor, and yourself. This simple statement, if practiced on a regular basis, will go far to eradicate evil—the violence, war, terrorism, crime, poverty, fear, and despair that hovers over your world like an impending storm cloud. At various times and places, this storm erupts, causing much anguish and hardship. Yet despite much effort by the factions involved, very little of anything positive is ever achieved to improve life as you know it.

This was not My plan for you. I have envisioned a much richer, more satisfying, and harmonious existence for My greatest creation, You! I bring you back to the reminder, love. Love me, love your neighbor, and love yourself! You cannot love any one of these three unless you know each one, and to do that, you must set aside time to be alone with each one.

My scribe had an awareness lesson last evening. After fifty-some odd years of being convinced that she didn't measure up—that she was not as smart, thin, or good a wife, mother, daughter, or friend as others—tonight, after several years of working directly with Me in prayer and meditation, a reality light bulb has come on in her heart. She has finally grasped the concept that others are not better than she is. She is as good as others are!

She has just let go of a worldly yardstick, realizing that using that yardstick ensures she will never measure up. Why? With that yardstick, she can never get it right, for that yardstick is always changing, day to day, year to year, or culture to culture. Her willingness to steadily plug away at developing a relationship with Me has begun the process of inner healing, one that cannot be achieved with any degree of success without My input.

Due to her efforts, she has begun to love Me. In so doing, she has also begun to experience this inner healing and is thus beginning to be able to accept and therefore love herself. The inevitable outcome of this process is to be able to love others. This will begin to change her world.

Are you catching My drift, precious friends? This process will work for you, your family, your community, your nation, and the world. If you love, you cannot hate. If you cannot hate, you foster healing and peace. If you foster peace, you hasten the arrival of My kingdom here on earth.

It is time to try something new, a different approach. What you have been doing for the last few thousand years has had limited success because, when what you want is not readily achievable, you revert to force. This will not work in the long run.

I have given you all free choice. You have been free to do it your way since I first put humans on earth. You are maturing, growing older. Take on the responsibility of your status as heirs of the Father's kingdom. Become an asset for success. Cease to be the excuse for failure. If you strive to love Me and yourself, automatically you will find yourself loving your neighbor and life!

My plans for you all are success, not failure.

0-0

SAME-SEX MARRIAGES

Dear God, it has been suggested that we write to our members of parliament, the prime minister, and anyone else who we feel might have some influence to object to the proposed discussion paper being presented in the legislature that wishes to make same-sex marriages, viable, and equal to heterosexual marriages.

In this last year, You have been asking me to give considerable thought to relationships and the importance of committed relationships, regardless of gender. We know that a loving and nurturing mother and father have so far outdistanced other situations as the most efficacious circumstances for raising children.

We also know that horrendous situations can be a reality in the heterosexual family setting. We know it is possible for one person to successfully raise several children; thus these children are exposed to only a male or female approach to nurturing and life lessons. If this is the case, is it not possible for two loving and committed persons of the same gender to successfully raise a child or children?

We truly are preoccupied with sex and sexuality, Lord. We are most easily offended by that which is sexual but seem to take much less offense to such things as violence, cruelty, murder, and mayhem. Many sigh with resignation when we hear of corporate wrongdoing.

Sometimes we might be coerced into opening our wallets to help feed the poor. We have little or no interest or compassion if prisoners riot over mistreatment in our jails. "They don't deserve to be treated with dignity. Look what they have done to society!"

But let one human being put his or her hand too close to a breast, a buttock, or a private part (as we don't even like to use the words *penis* or *vagina*), and many gasp in horror. We are sexual beings, created that way by You, yet after several thousands of years, we still do not feel comfortable with this reality.

Dear God, Creator of the universe, loving and understanding parent, would You please give us some wisdom on how to handle this latest ripple in our societal development?

ೞ

Annie, write this.

GG I know you feel inadequate to be writing anything definitive on this subject, but you are not the source of what you write. I am! Many factors can be presented in a debate of this nature. There are religious, social, legal, and hetero and homosexual arguments. It could be argued from the standpoint of what is best for the preservation of a particular religious, social, or individual perspective.

There is no simple answer here, but there is one simple principle that, if considered, will go far to help you to develop appropriate legislation that will ensure the dignity and welfare of all involved. And that principle is love. I am not speaking of sexual attachment; I am speaking of respectful, responsible commitment of one human being to another. If each and every one of you lived a life that was committed to the respectful and responsible treatment of your fellow human beings, this sexuality factor would no longer be an issue.

"But what about procreation?" some of you cry.

Just as many babies are being conceived as ever, but you are either killing them off or allowing them to be killed off (abortion). If there are just as many conceptions as ever, one might observe that My initial plan for keeping the human race around has not run aground. Your responsible and committed respect for yourselves has run aground.

The issues here should not be, "Should there be legislation in favor of same-sex marriages?" or "Should same-sex marriages be seen to be on equal footing with marriages of the opposite sex?" Might not the best way to come to this debate be, "How can we best create the optimum environment for the raising of children and a respectful and responsible community that meets others' needs (not the self-righteousness of a few)?"

Every human being needs to love and be loved. Who loves you is not as important as the fact that **someone** loves you. Keep this fact in mind as you plan your future's societal norms. Many of the ones you have chosen to date have not been serving you well.

I have given you free choice in all matters. This means you have been permitted to have made mistakes, but you have also been given the choice to improve on those past choices. You are here on earth to perfect, to be ever evolving into a closer and closer reflection of That which created you.

Yours truly,

O-O

A CRIME OR AN ACCIDENT WAITING TO HAPPEN

*D*ear God, this question pertains to the trial of the American airmen who accidentally fired on friendly ground troops, resulting in the deaths of some. The American military is reported to be planning long jail sentences. The families of the airmen are shocked that their own country would treat them with such severity. When asked if he felt that he could ever forgive these pilots, a survivor of the attack haltingly said, "Maybe ... well, yes ... but first I have to get through the shock and grief that I am feeling."

Dear Lord, You know how and why this happened. Lives have been unalterably changed because of these events. If these circumstances are dealt with in the prescribed manner, very little good is likely to emerge. How should the people of a loving God resolve this issue?

ଔ

Ann, thank you for asking.

GG This was not a malicious act. Age, experience, excitement undergirded with fear, and the mind-set of the modern world played a significant role in this incident. The persons and their personal circumstances, their training, and their weaponry did the rest, death and destruction waiting for the perfect moment, be it with friend or foe.

If you train people to overcome their natural aversion to killing one another, enable them to do it from such a distance that they never see the resultant horror, and give them the authority to discharge these weapons, the result will be death, plainly and simply.

The airmen whose task it is to kill indiscriminately, never having to see the dimension of human suffering that they wreak, have finally been given an opportunity to hear the stories and see the anguish that is the result of modern war. And incidentally, this sort of tragedy gets played out on a daily basis all over the world. This could happen in any country with any military servicemen. Who is to blame? Who should be court-martialed and jailed?

Would it be those who design and manufacture weapons of destruction; governments that buy these weapons; the military that condones their use and trains the men to use them; the leaders who incite hatred; the newspapers that spread hatred; people who find justification for war and killing; or people who object to all of the above and say nothing?

I say this not to condemn you but to enlighten you. All these years of experience should be enough feedback to tell you that this kind of activity does not solve problems. It is a Band-Aid response. It is schoolyard mentality.

As most small boys eventually cease to solve their problems with schoolyard fights, so too should the human race cease to solve their particular needs assessments with strong-arm tactics. There are alternatives. Wisdom, compassion, and knowledge of the other guy— his culture, needs, and concerns—will go a long way in making war and weaponry obsolete.

Your futuristic writings of advanced cultures that no longer go to war are merely the statements of your prophets. Only You decide how quickly that evolution occurs.

0-0

FEAR KEEPS YOU AND I APART

*D*ear God, I am feeling frustrated. You seem to have been leading me through flight class. You have placed books, situations, thoughts, and meditations before me that cause me to begin to believe that You want us to soar. A wonderful sense of excitement growing inside says, "Maybe there is more to life than to just get through it." You have allowed me to sense the mystical. You have reminded me again and again of Jesus' words, "This and more you shall do!"

I get revved up and excited about it all, and I go to share only to run into those who want to go back to the silence, the whispers, the incense, the sacred, the ritual, the obedience, the fear. You have taught me to enjoy Your company, to discuss, to complain, to listen, to love you, and, through it all, to feel totally loved and accepted by You. You seem to encourage soaring!

The old way, that silent awe with its whispers and obedience, now seems confining, limiting, and unfamiliar. This chasm that is evident in my spirituality, Lord, is causing confusion. If I share, I estrange certain others. If I keep it to myself, I'm defeating the purpose of the journey. Lord, Your insight is required.

Annava, write this.

To all My children, My offspring, My greatest creations,

GG I am the Creator of the universe and the Creator of all that is. And I wish to tell you a truth. Fear of Me prevents you from knowing and loving Me and all I offer.

A child who is taught to be obedient through fear of punishment is unable to experience life to the fullest. Depending on future circumstances, that child will either experience life's journey in a limited way or in breaking free of what he or she perceives to be very stifling controls, might cast all caution aside and live life recklessly.

Fear is prohibitive. Its purpose is to control. In the very young, it may prevent them from getting lost or injured. To be afraid of lighting matches or walking across a very busy street is a healthy fear for a small child. It is not a healthy fear for a teenager or adult. Fear can provide a person with a healthy respect for inherent dangers in any situation, but it is not meant to cripple one's experiences of life. Fear has also come to play a large role in your spiritual lives and your inability or difficulty in developing a relationship with your God, Me!

I do not wish to be feared. I do not wish for you to be so in awe of Me that We never come face-to-face. Have you been led to believe that I demand awe, reverence, praise, and so on? When you truly know Me, these things will become a given, but only because you have come to comprehend who and what I am, not because I need or demand your awe, reverence, or praise.

The only thing I would truly like from you is your love, and I can only hope to acquire that if you come to know and trust Me. I am telling you these things, Annie, because you listen to Me and are slowly beginning to trust

Me. And I trust in your/our ability to write down these words so others may hear them as well.

I desire and look for relationship and love with each soul that I personally put into place on this earth.

0-0

NOW OR IN GOD'S TIME!

*D*ear God, about ten years ago, I was asking You about the Gulf War. Now another war is raging with Iraq. Their leader is still Saddam Hussein.

I have heard the arguments for and against war. As of today, apparently allies have shot down a British plane. The United Nations are divided over their support of the Americans. We Canadians have chosen to stay put and not support the effort at this time, yet we did send troops off to Afghanistan to free up the American troops there so they could join their countrymen in Iraq.

Lord, we truly do not know all the truth. I believe we hear only what the powers-that-be want us to hear. We do not know how much of what we hear is truth or merely some zealous reporters wanting to sell their stories. War was apparently condoned by You if we are to believe literally certain stories in the Old Testament.

How else could this situation have been resolved, Lord? How does one deal with someone who terrorizes his own people, who seems to be motivated strictly by ego? I cannot say he is mad, but he certainly seems to be blinded to common sense. We do not know this man, only some of his actions. And those actions seem to be prophesying that, if he is not stopped soon, he will eventually be behind attacks of a much broader and deadlier sort than occurred on September 11.

Thank You for listening.

☙

Annava, write this.

GG I hear your confusion and your frustration. I know what it is like to experience deep concern about where people are going, knowing you will not make any impact (yet) to alter what seems to be the inevitable.

0-0

☙

There was no further response to the above concern, and now maybe a month later, maybe I can see why. Maybe this particular Iraqi leader needed to be deposed. The news broadcast at that time by the Iraqi television network was showing hundreds of their people all deliriously supportive of Saddam Hussein and all passionately hating the Western world. Here we are a month later, an invasion and ousting all but over. And now we are seeing the Iraqi people smashing the effigies of Saddam and apparently grateful to be relieved of this despot.

Truly, how do we know when what we are presented with in news coverage is actual fact or merely something dreamed up by certain factions? When this latest war began and all sorts of predictions were being bandied about, I opted to absent myself from the details, although I certainly heard those details that had caught the attention of friends and family. I could not stop the invasion whether I agreed with it or not. I could do nothing but pray that God would turn another human decision into something positive.

Maybe it is too early to tell, but one thing is certain. A suppressed people has been liberated from a cruel despot, and hopefully this is a good thing.

I am not a political analyst. I am not even an informed reader. I would love to be able to skillfully write a succinct analysis of this last month and be able to prove beyond a shadow of a doubt that what the West did was right or good and what was going on in Iraq was wrong or bad. But I don't believe that is why God has me writing, so I will leave this pen for Him to take it from here.

But apparently, not at this moment!

LEARNING TO ACCEPT RESPONSIBILITY

Annie, you are concerned that the writing of your story is slowing down the writing of this book. Have you felt called to write in this book?

○○

Not until just now, Lord.

○○

Then what is the problem? Do you write for yourself or at My encouragement? You have never refused to write any time I have asked you. We have no particular deadline to meet. Be at peace, child. All is progressing on plan.

GG You are feeling that maybe the widespread power blackout in the northeast region of North America last Thursday (August 15, 2003) might be a topic that could be addressed here. At this point, the news media and the politicians are the only people who have been heard from. The people who have the knowledge to figure out why it happened and what to do about it are busy doing just that.

You live in the heartland of where it's all happening. It is understandable that this is where a power shortage would occur. It will be dealt with, and you will all move on. But it is a wake-up call to the powers-that-be to set in place some priorities.

Progress and discovery are good, but never at the expense of the common good. The demands of a few should never outweigh the well-being of the general public. It is unwise to create a system that does not have a contingency plan should the primary program fail for one reason or another. It is wiser to have in place the ability to provide essential services in several ways. The backup system may never be as efficient as the latest technology, but at least the essentials are available. You, as humans, must never let technology become more important than existence on earth. The day-to-day reality of looking after body and soul must always remain a top priority.

What is the importance of discovering a drug that overcomes all illness if there is no one on earth to use it? What is the point of learning what else is out there in the universe if you have not taken care of the basics here on earth? If you develop the capacity to find and settle other worlds, should you not have a better running model to start with? Should you not channel your energies into improving and correcting what has been learned by trial and error here before heading out to start anew with insufficient wisdom and knowledge?

Many of you behave like the child presented with a variety of new toys for a particular birthday. Once explored, you leave the objects just where you lost interest and move on to something else. You do not clean up after yourselves or leave things ready for the next person or persons to fully utilize that of which you have lost interest. Learn to be responsible. By all means, explore your world and discover all I have packed into it. But as you open each new gift, be sure that you have discovered all that is in the box, the responsibility of possession, and how best to leave the gift for the use of others.

ANN MONSTER

There is much gratification at being in the forefront of where it's happening, but there is also much responsibility to administer wisely. Remember, if I knew that you could never achieve the wisdom to utilize one of My gifts, I would never allow you to discover it.

All that you achieve is from Me. You receive because I love you. Ask for the wisdom to utilize all that I allow you to achieve with the skill and dignity inherent in the offspring of the Creator.

0-0

THE MECHANICS OF HEALING A FALTERING MARRIAGE

*D*ear God, a family incident has unsettled me a little, and it is not even the immediate family. At this point, it looks like an unpleasant, marriage deterioration with both sides telling their stories from their own perspectives with much blaming and finger-pointing. The observers, for the most part, are trying to be fair and understanding to both parties. Lord, I think this causes me to feel unsettled, for once again, anger is a frequently visible factor in this particular situation. Anger is an emotion with which I have always struggled. I have the feeling that You wish to address this issue in this manuscript. The pen is Yours.

ଓ

Thank you, Ann. I know how difficult it is for you to air family laundry, but this is an issue that many families face today.

GG When relationships begin to break down, people's coping skills are truly put to the test. Most people cope reasonably well with situations that have a clear focus, a straightforward solution, and a short-term resolution period.

Ann Monster

In a relationship resolution, it is always difficult to find the true causes for the dissolution. There is seldom an easy solution, and a positive outcome is dependent on the attitudes and ethics of the two parties that were the cause of the problem in the first place.

This statement is not meant to point more fingers, depress you, or ride roughshod over any hope you might have for a happy outcome. What it is meant to do is to help the participants or observers to put hope back into a practical and workable framework.

Many factors have gone into creating this situation. When all aspects of the situation have been revealed, each participant or observer has a choice as to how he or she views those aspects, and all will have to accept that resolution may be a slow and painful process toward healing.

The inner healing of the individuals involved is the key to a successful outcome, which does not necessarily result in the couple staying together. But if I am asked into the equation, the chances of that are greatly increased. I say this because, on occasion, marriage is entered into by a person or persons who are inadequately prepared to cope with the responsibility of the calling. Marriage requires commitment to others, first to the mate and second to the offspring. Needless to say, whichever one of these takes priority may depend on the ages of either of the above mentioned.

Marriages seldom grow into strong unions when one or both partners are frequently self-focused. Marriage, by definition, is union, meaning the melding of separate persons into oneness. That cannot happen when the parties in question are unable to focus on the needs and desires of the other. This is not to say that self-actualization cannot be achieved in marriage. It's just the opposite with the assistance and support of the other. Each is assisted in the attainment of his or her own personal goal.

Marriage dissolution, more often than not, brings with it hurt, pain, and disappointment. What may also rear the ugly heads are anger, resentment, blame, shame, downright hatred, and a desire to get even. Under these circumstances, any kind of resolution is slowed or stopped, for these types of feelings do not promote clear, common sense, decision making.

Once the hurts begin to undercut the trust that hopefully existed at one time in the relationship, then all manner of thoughts can begin to work on the minds of the aggrieved parties. This is destructive, for it causes a willingness to believe the worst, to see treachery in every act and word, and to drive both parties farther and farther apart. Unfortunately, the fallout from a venomous situation can also affect children, families, and friends, causing people to take sides or abandon the couple altogether.

When baiting, goading, physical or verbal abuse, or threats become the norm, it is time for the parties to keep their distance and each gets individual help to assist each of them to decide what he or she wishes to do. Do they want the relationship to heal? Do they desire to work at it? Are they willing to acknowledge that there could be fault on both sides? Do they care how the other makes out after the breakup, or do they just expect to walk away and start somewhere else?

If a person does not resolve the issues that caused the problems in the first place, the same issues will continue to haunt every successive relationship he or she pursues. These experiences occur because something needs to be learned (healed). Until the person or persons choose to learn the lessons that are being offered, they will continue to be presented with the same lesson until the eureka moment occurs and they finally understand.

0-0

WHEN PRAYING FOR OTHERS

*D*ear God, what's going on? I was supposed to take Liz communion and pray over her in hospital this morning. It's snowing, and the car won't start. Are You trying to tell me something? Should I not have suggested praying over her? We have done this for others. Am I not supposed to do this alone? Bert has the flu. He cannot come. Have I made a move without Your permission? Lord, please advise.

ૐ

Annie, it's okay. I am not angry with you, but I did need you to write about this before you go. Remember the prodding to write last night?

ૐ

Yes, Lord. I'm sorry. I'm not always sure if it's You or if it's just wishful thinking on my part.

ૐ

GG Annie, whenever you pray for someone, especially in a situation like Liz's (terminal cancer), you must allow the Spirit to do the asking. Because I have not given you the gift of being able to discern a person's future, it is better to allow the Holy Spirit to do the asking. The Holy Spirit knows

My will for each soul. This way, all that the person needs is asked for, and anyone who hears the proceedings is never able to say that I do not answer prayers. In many hearts (including yours when it comes to healing), I have little enough credibility without estranging those who may still have hope in Me.

By all means, pray over Liz. Just pray in tongues, and wait to see what I will do, even if you too doubt Me. I love you, Annie. I understand that you doubt your own faith to bring about healing, but it is not your faith. But My love brings healing, any healing, and your belief in My love for each of you. That I have given you, a belief in My love for each of you. Take your own mind there when you pray in tongues and leave the rest up to Me.

0-0

LOVE HEALS

*D*ear Papa, Your last message—the visit with Liz and her statement that she figured she was suffering because she had such a wonderful, fulfilling, and advantaged life and now had to pay for it—this has triggered some memories.

I remember when our friend Bob was dying. He seemed to project a similar reflection. Because he had been quite a hellion when he was younger, he had to pay for it now. I can remember that You told me to tell him to concentrate on Your love for him, not on his past. He didn't seem to be able to forgive himself. He died peacefully and quickly in a very short period of time.

This is the second time I have been in a relationship with someone who is dying where You have stressed the importance of their focus on Your love for them. Is there more to be said here, Lord, or am I reading more into this than needs be?

ॐ

Annie, I thank you for this opportunity to get down on paper the importance of My love for any one of you.

GG You have heard the statement, "God is love." In dire situations, most of you will call out desperately to Me, knowing innately that, when you feel at your wit's end, when nothing else has helped, or when you are facing death and don't feel ready, God working a miracle is the only solution. I have programmed this innate knowledge into your systems as a fail-safe, meaning that, even if you do not know Me, do not want to know Me, or have rejected Me, you will automatically reach for Me when your spirit knows it needs Me, the source of all good.

If I have placed this system within you in case of emergencies, imagine what a relationship with Me on a regular basis might be like! If I am the sort of God who would provide all souls with an emergency resource whether they knew Me or not, loved Me or not, or even just acknowledged Me, what would I be likely to do for the soul who had tried to do the best he or she could with what life had given to them?

Annie, I have been given many names by many different peoples. Some are awe-filled, others are very specific, and a few are intimate. But when you wish to describe Me truly, I am love. My love heals all wounds. My love cures all illness. My love accomplishes the impossible, but only if it is received.

Annie, if you are thirsty and someone offers you a drink, your thirst cannot and will not be relieved if you will not reach out, take the glass, and drink from it. If someone hands you a gift but you do not open it, you will never know what was offered to you, let alone enjoy the benefits of its possession.

It is the same with My love. I have said again and again that I love each and every one of you as if You were the only soul that I ever created. Many of you have heard this but pay little heed. You compare My love to parental love, which is seldom unconditional. You compare my love to a spouse's love, which is rarely unconditional. You compare it to your own ability to love, which is hardly ever unconditional. My love is always unconditional! You mistakenly compare My ability to love with the world's ability to love. The world loves conditionally.

Many of you are hung up on not being worthy! Think about this one! I created you! Would I have created something that was unworthy of Me? Could I, God, have created something that was unworthy of Me?

When I gave you free choice, was I so shortsighted as to think that you would all choose the correct choice? The word choice means just that. You have options! Yes, some are wiser than others are, but they are still choices. Yes, you may reap the rewards of less than wise choices, but that is why I initially gave you some guidelines (what some call the Ten Commandments), just so you did not have to learn everything the hard way.

I love you regardless of your choices. When I poured Myself into human form and walked the earth for thirty-three years, I condensed My directives into a very simple rule. Love me, your neighbor, and yourself. There's that word "love" again! It all boils down to love—your love for Me, your love for your neighbor, and your love for yourself—but the most powerful, awesome, and miraculous love of all is My love for you!

When Jesus healed, He healed with love. When I heal, I heal with love. When those of you who have been given the gift of healing and are using it (in other words, they opened their gift), you do so with My love. My love heals those who accept and actively acknowledge the potency of My love for them. When you accept and receive My love, it will heal you.

Trust in My love for you.

0-0

HIV/AIDS

*P*apa, there is much controversy surrounding what our approach should be for the hundreds of thousands of people in Africa who are struggling with HIV/AIDS. I know what I think, but my upbringing colors that. Papa, what is Your wisdom for us as we reach out to help our brothers and sisters with humanity?

☙

Annie, thank you for the opportunity to speak to the hearts of all My children, those who are suffering and those who choose to help.

GG First and foremost, I love you all. Do not look upon this problem as God's punishment meted out upon an abomination but as a human dilemma, allowed by Me, to assist mankind to grow in love, compassion, and wisdom.

When a fire is raging out of control, do everything in your power to control the spread, even as you are attempting to put it out. At no time would anyone consider not helping because the causative factor had been carelessness.

When people are starving, do you decide whether or not to help them based on your interpretation of their responsibility? My dearest children, these brothers and sisters who are suffering have not had the advantages, educations, and opportunities that have been made available to you, the decision makers, in an affluent world.

Do not judge others by comparing their behavior to what you yourself would do under similar circumstances. You are worlds apart in your attitudes, needs, expectations, and hopes. You cannot begin to comprehend from where they are coming because most of you have never walked a day (let alone a lifetime) in their shoes.

Cease your judgments, and do all that your present-day knowledge would suggest that you do to stem the spread of this contagion. I refer not only to the physical condition but to the self-righteous attitudes that persist, enabling you to turn away from the orphaned, the terrified, the sick, and the dying. When you have done all that needs to be done for those who are suffering, then and only then is the time to instruct gently and clearly as to how to avoid any future problem.

This is My unconditional approach to you all. Do not allow conditional thinking to set the standard of world behavior.

You are all My children. Do Me proud!

0-0

ERADICATING POVERTY

Dear God, Yesterday I drove to Toronto with family and friends, took in a wonderful play, had two meals, stayed in contact with family back here by cell phone, and had enough cash on hand to grab a cab to get us to the theatre on time. It was an enjoyable day, and even though driving was a bit stressful on the way home, we arrived safely. Thank You.

End of story? Not so.

Papa, three scenes are sticking in my head. The first was seeing a man crawl into a structure of some sort that was erected under the Gardener Expressway (the downtown Toronto overpass). The second was a man with a homeless sign standing outside the theatre when we came out. The third was a young girl, face and fingers pink from the cold, who asked if I might have anything that I could spare.

My mind is spinning with the disgrace and shame I feel being part of this affluent culture that could accept people lying in heaps of dirty old materials on freezing, filthy street corners while meticulously dressed men and women hurry by. Papa, I realize that many of us hurry by because giving a bit of money here or there does not change the lot of the homeless. There are those who have the mind-set that the homeless are just lazy. If they wanted to work, they could!

There are so many variables in our lives, Papa. I see these people, and something aches inside me for them, but also for those of us who would like to help but don't know how. If there is a way to provide them with shelter, food, and caring (as these places are available in some communities) but also to help them to regain a sense of worth and some independence, please inspire us now. The pen is Yours.

ଓ

Annie, thank you for seeing, caring, and listening.

GG You have heard it said before, "The poor, you will always have with you." The rich need the poor to keep them honest and focused on productive uses of their monies.

I have no difficulty with the pursuit of money. What I do want to address is a pursuit of money for the sake of bigger bank balances, greater personal wealth and pleasure than the next person and ever-increasing power, particularly at the expense of others. A life lived to excess is a life wasted.

There is so much more to life than the acquisition of things. Life is about participation in this world. As you are all One with Me (whether you believe in Me or not), this life I have entrusted to you is yours to use for the betterment of all. I give you gifts and talents, and life gives you the opportunities to maximize those gifts and talents to make the world a better place for all its inhabitants, thus leading following generations forward, toward the arrival of My kingdom here on earth.

This scribe of Mine started out her life in the absence of love. That deficit left her broken and needy. Like most of you, she pressed on in spite of the shortcomings because that was all with which she was familiar. It was only years later that she finally realized how important those beginnings really were. *Only later did she recognize the jewel that she has come to possess just because of those original circumstances. Like so many, you have discovered that, if it had not been for the struggles and hardships of earlier years, none of what you have accomplished to date would have occurred.*

Everyone has choices, the rich and poor alike. I came so you could have life in abundance. Abundance means different things to different people. I see some of you are enormously wealthy, yet inside you are unhappy and wasting away. I see others who are just getting by, but inside you are peaceful and growing. It is all a matter of inner or spiritual growth and maturity.

The infant cries for its own perceived needs, whereas the matured parent puts aside its own needs for that of the child. Young people might have difficulty sharing (their toys), whereas adults probably are able to understand the benefits of sharing. Caring for others in the community is a sign of maturity and responsibility. I ask you to use the gifts and talents I have given to you to provide for yourselves, yes, but to also put back into the system some of what you have gleaned.

All humans need air to breathe, food to eat, and warmth. This is just to stay alive. Yes, there are facilities that provide those things in most of your big cities, so why are there still people living on the streets? Because the facilities seldom provide that one other commodity that is so important to the human heart- **dignity and self-worth**.

Be very slow to judge what you perceive to be failures of society. Do not pass them off as dross because life did not hand them all they needed to succeed. Do not dismiss them because they appear to not have made the most of what they had.

Believe it or not, buried under the lean-to shack, the dirty blanket, and shabby clothes is great wealth. I am asking certain of you to become miners, to discover the hidden gifts, the ideas, ingenuity, and humor that lay just below the bedraggled surfaces of these awesome human beings.

Yes, feed them, and give them a safe, warm place to sleep and some decent food, but do not stop there. Help them to recognize their own talents, to plumb the depths of their own experiential knowledge. Ask them about what does and does not work—what they need to make it work, what could be done better, and what helps them to achieve a degree of independence.

To get your answers, talk to those who are still maintaining their independence by sleeping in cardboard boxes under bridges. Many of you who have achieved success are hard-pressed to ask someone else to give you something. You would rather pay for it. Do you not realize that self-reliance is desperately alive in many of these precious souls who have no desire to be needy?

There are ways to develop community living situations in which these homeless people can become self-sufficient and productive. Lose your guilt complexes, and put My wisdom, your ingenuity, and their experience to work, and you will have something that will go far in revitalizing communities all over the world.

The only reason that this has not happened to date is because too many of the people who could so easily design the programs pour their energies and talents into the pursuit of increasing bank balances.

There are those of you who will read this and know that I am speaking to you. Listen to what I am telling you in your heart. I will help you every step of the way. There will be people who will give generously to something they know will bring about self-sufficiency and returns to the community.

Do not try to do this without the input of those who have more experience than any university could ever teach! The homeless are going to become the resources that will make it work. Do not do it for them. Do it with them!

0-0

RETHINKING SEXUALITY

Today, I tried to allow the Spirit to take me where It led me. Sexuality and reproduction were the focus. I leave the pen to You, God, for I am still trying to collect my thoughts on the concepts that You have presented, and I am concerned at my lack of ability to present these concepts clearly and accurately.

☙

Annie, Thank you for listening.

You are not the first to hear these concepts, but you are one of the first to write them down in language that the average human being will be able to comprehend.

GG I said to you, "The seat of the soul lays centered in the reproductive organs of the human body."

Your initial reaction to this concept was shock, then disgust, rejection, and finally doubt. You found it difficult to believe that it was I, God, Spirit, Christ, and Savior, speaking to you or, to put it more accurately, conveying a clearer understanding of a divine concept. I will explain.

For too long, mankind has been preoccupied with the feel of sexuality. I'm not saying that there is anything wrong with the feel of sexuality.

How could there be? I created it! What I am saying is that to merely feel sexuality, to be preoccupied with feeling the feelings, and to never fully understand the divine effect is like being satisfied to merely smell the aroma of freshly baked apple pie without ever actually consuming any.

I put mankind on earth to love—Me, their fellow man, and themselves. That is a very basic understanding of My purpose for putting you here. The longer you are here, the greater should become your comprehension of your potential, your power, and your responsibility. Because I knew that it would take mankind a while to develop, grow, and mature, I made sure that the feel of sexuality would ensure the continuation of the race until it got up to speed.

As you enter what is referred to as the third millennium, I desire that mankind begin to understand the bigger picture of sexuality. I will start with an analogy: When children are little, you warn them against playing with matches because there is an inherent danger of getting burned themselves or causing damage to others as well. Even though you warn them against the use of matches because they do not, as yet, have the necessary wisdom to use them wisely, there is nothing inherently wrong with the lighting of a match.

Within mankind, a mind-set has evolved that has kept the experiencing of sexuality at an immature level. I am not blaming you for your present interpretation. A natural evolution of comprehension has long been stagnated by the preoccupation of sin associated with the feelings. The feelings are not sinful. What you do with the feelings can remain at the immature level, or you can leave yourselves open to accept and experience My greatest gift to My most astounding creations, the ability to create another human being, the consuming or consummation of the gift.

It is time for the old perception of sexuality to be exposed and corrected. Pass on a healthier attitude to the coming generations. It is time to be honest with young people as they enter their teenage years. Be open about how wonderful it may feel and what causes it to feel so good but how difficult it can be on a person who is not developed or mature enough to know when and how to experience it. Tell them of the responsibility! The silence, shame, fear, ignorance, and disgust, to say nothing of the immature fixation on merely the feel, does much to keep the problem self-perpetuating.

I ask you to give this idea time, time to become understood, considered, reassessed, and accepted. If you ask Me to be part of the thinking process, you will make great progress. If you do not, you will merely stay where you are, smelling and never tasting. I did not intend that one of My greatest gifts to you would become one of your greatest stumbling blocks.

You are all called to love. Upgrade your vocabulary to define love distinctly. To love sports, the theatre or travel is not the same as loving a human being. Loving a neighbor is not the same as loving a spouse. Become aware of the ideas that exist in your head, the feelings that exist in your heart, and the awesome potential to create within your person. Develop a mature responsibility for all aspects of your life, and teach it to your offspring.

The ultimate potential of mankind will be achieved when you truly comprehend that the seat of the soul lays centered in the reproductive organs of the human body.

0-0

CR

Dear God, It has been a while since we've worked on this manuscript. A recent ruling by the Canadian government, giving gay people the legal right to have their unions recognized, has many groups up in arms. I have wrestled with my thoughts, but I want to hear Your input. All You have been presenting to me in so many different ways has given me a lot to think about. I am ready to listen and to transcribe Your insights.

☙

Annava,

GG You are ready, and so am I! Where is it written, "Thou shalt not love"? Where is it stated that it is wrong to dedicate your life to the care and concern for another human being? Where is it written that I frown on the expression of that love through intimate touch and sexual expression?

For much of the history of the civilized world (note the word civilized), the people inhabiting it have had a preoccupation with sexuality and a predisposition of seeing it as sinful. Even between male and female, there has been a tendency to view any aspect of it as marital duty, the pleasure component of which is not to be discussed or enjoyed. Then on the other hand, there are those who indulge themselves in sexual activity without ever taking responsibility for their pleasure-seeking pursuits. Sexual gratification or sexuality that is devoid of love is an irresponsible approach and bespeaks immaturity and self-centeredness.

☙

Lord, the adjective *lewd* is probably the word that most people associate with sexuality and sin. The dictionary definition expresses it as inclined to, characterized by, or inciting to lust or lechery, obscenity, or indecency.

A MATURE AND RESPONSIBLE APPROACH TO SEXUALITY

I'm pretty sure that I know the meaning of lust and lechery, but just to be absolutely sure, lechery is defined as free or excessive sexual indulgence. Lust is defined with more ambiguity. The first definition is sexual desire or appetite; uncontrolled or illicit sexual desire or appetite, lecherousness; a passionate or overmastering desire; ardent enthusiasm, zest, relish; pleasure or delight, desire, inclination, wish; to have a strong sexual desire; or to have a passionate yearning or desire, having a strong or excessive craving.

Lord, I've taken the time to put these definitions down here because, when I looked them up for my own edification, I was surprised how words that we have so frequently associated with sin are not necessarily defined that way. I am not trying to condone lewd behavior, but when does the natural and beautiful sexual desire that one human being can have for another, become sin?

○ঽ

GG Firstly, I would like to suggest that the terminology "sin" be replaced with immature, uninformed, or irresponsible choice. As you have acknowledged above, it is very hard to separate natural lust or enthusiasm for sexual activity from lewd conduct as obviously frowned upon in Scripture. Lewd conduct or immature or irresponsible choice is probably best explained as sexual activity with a stranger; forced sexual activity with another; sexual activity with nonhumans (animals); sexual activity intended to cause pain, shame, degradation, injury, or punishment; or sexual gratification achieved with the innocent.

Personal sexual development is rarely something over which a human being has control. If early human sexual development gets skewed even a little, it can affect the developing adult, causing possible lifelong difficulties in sexual responsiveness.

If sexual development gets seriously skewed in a youngster or teen, it can greatly affect their ability to handle their sexuality in adulthood. If his or her behavior as an adult manifests inappropriate sexual activity, one has to ask, "Is he or she sinning or acting out of brokenness?" This is the reason behind turning from judgment to awareness and compassion.

Why are we discussing all this at such length? Because you humans have an unhealthy preoccupation with sexuality. When I say unhealthy, I mean just that! I am not saying it is sinful. I am saying it is unhealthy. You see sin lurking behind every door, action, or thought. You see sexual pleasure as sin. You see "lust" as a sinful word. There are those of you who are unable to call various parts of the body by their anatomical names. There are those of you who see nakedness as sin.

Yet the advertising community recognizes this preoccupation full well and uses it to the maximum. Every imaginable product or service is in some way tinged with the suggestion that having or using the product for sale will improve the buyer's sexual experience even if one just happens to come across the seller's advertisement. Any newspaper, magazine, billboard, or television advertising is perpetually bombarding the viewer with the subliminal suggestion that sexuality is about the only facet of life that has any importance.

It is general knowledge that, if children are told they cannot have something, it will immediately become the only thing that they do want. How often, as parents, have you given into a child's tantrum about being denied something only to discover that, once they have it, they soon lose interest? This scribe used to notice her very young grandchildren bickering over what each had been given. They only appeared to be dissatisfied with what they had received when they realized the other one had received something different. Reversing what each had, brought momentary satisfaction, but within minutes, they would realize that they no longer possessed what they were originally given, and they would want back what they had so readily discarded. This is a typical trait of childhood. Unfortunately many adults fail to grow out of it, carrying a resultant inability to be satisfied with anything for any great length of time.

If people did not perceive sexuality as sin—desire, thoughts, and feelings as sin—there would be much less preoccupation with it. If you accepted it as a natural aspect of life, just like getting hungry or tired, a lot of your social problems would disappear.

I remind you of the original native peoples who, in most cases, wore very little clothing, if any, unless survival in colder climates demanded it. These people had no contact with civilization or the social mores that were developing elsewhere. They experienced no shame about their bodies. Breasts, genitals, and buttocks were just as ordinary as hands, feet, legs, arms, and heads.

The civilizations have created a skewed normalcy. I remind you that, even in the animal world, sexual behavior between like genders is quite evident. Being held, touched, patted, cuddled, or groomed by another generates a sense of well-being, and so it does for humans.

This is another area that the Western civilizations have twisted pathetically, the whole concept of touch. Because a small percentage of the population has acted out of its brokenness, you have enacted laws that *prevent all touching of any kind in all situations dealing with children. Because another sector of the population has acted out of its brokenness, you have enacted laws that make it extremely difficult for many other parents to satisfactorily achieve a degree of discipline and responsibility in their families. You look at society, believing that all is deteriorating but having not the eyes to see that your own fears are the causative factors perpetuating this illusion.*

As I have said before, I created each of you with a sexual component, not just for procreation but to enable you to enhance the living of life through the wonderful gift of touch. Sexuality is just one of many ways to touch. Sexuality is, in essence, merely one of many aspects of life. Many of you have given it ascendancy over everything else. This is partly natural, for it brings humans together to populate the world. After that purpose has been achieved, it is normal for sexuality to move back into a position of equality with all other aspects of life. Unfortunately many in the Western culture fall for the deceptive belief that, unless you are still sexually preoccupied, you have passed your prime, become unimportant, or are out of the loop.

My dear friends, open the eyes of your hearts. Cease your judgments. That is My domain! Begin to look at your belief systems and, in particular, your sexual mores. Do you really believe that I would create anything as exciting, pleasurable, or preoccupying as sexuality and then condemn you for finding it exciting, pleasurable, and preoccupying?

If I intended it only for procreation, why is it that a baby is not always the result of intercourse? Yes, I know all about cycles. Remember that I did design it! So why would I put a reasonably predictable rhythm into the pattern, to tease you or to give you choices, that is, number of children, sexual release without the burden of more children, or, if fertility is a problem, the ability to work out optimum times.

As I have asked before, if sexual climax is only a side effect of attempting to procreate, then why did I make it possible for a person to achieve orgasm by himself or herself? Do you truly believe that is the sort of entity I am, one who would create something so wonderful and so hard to resist and then tell you not to use it unless you are procreating but do not enjoy it! I have seen many humans function like that, but I do not!

If an orgasm is only for procreation, why is it so effective in relieving stress and tension, helping an overwrought person to actually drift off to sleep? Why is it able to deepen a relationship? Why is it able to infuse a sense of self-esteem and being treasured?

If sexuality were presented to young people with openness, respect, and responsibility, many of the problems inherent in the teenage years would become a thing of the past. In adulthood, sexuality is usually an integral part of being human. Celibacy should be a personal choice, not something imposed by others. If a human being willingly forgoes intimate relationship in his or her life, so be it. I gave everyone free choice, and I will respect your choice. For those who do choose celibacy, please thoroughly explore your reasons for doing so and ask for the wisdom of the Holy Spirit to guide you.

If two people are truly committed to one another, I see it as their responsibility to decide how that caring might manifest itself. It is no one else's business!

If love is present, then so am I, and that is all that matters.

0-0

REINCARNATION: QUESTIONS AND ANSWERS

*D*ear God, It has been quite a while since this manuscript has been touched. What with working to get the third book published and writing the biographical one, this volume has been sitting on the back shelf. Assuming You are the stimulus for all my writing and the presenter of all the books I read that stimulate my thought and meditative processes, I sense this morning that the topic of reincarnation is to be addressed.

After all these years, God, I still wonder about using this vessel as Your voice, Your instruction, Your wisdom. I feel so inadequate, and the more that I read, I consider there are many writers out there who are much better at presenting grand concepts and scientific discovery. My brain seems to be forever trying to comprehend why we are here on earth and what You want or would like us to do while we are here.

In the last year or so, I have been reading such authors as David Hawkins, Eckhart Tolle, Diarmuid O'Murchu, the *Course in Miracles*, and parts of the Kabbalah. Lord, there is so much thought-provoking material here, concepts that cause us to attempt to think more clearly about our beginnings here on earth, our growth, our failures, our knowledge, and our ignorance (limited consciousness).

So many souls come into the world with such great potential, and yet so many leave, appearing to have made little or no progress toward perfection. Do we truly keep coming back, trying to make some headway? Do You have some place where we can work out our perfection if we were unsuccessful here? Do we get punished for our failure? Is there a whispered "but" at the end of Your declaration of Your unconditional love for us? The pen is Yours, Papa.

ଔ

Precious scribe, please write the following.

GG It is time for mankind to embrace its reality. It is time for the awesomeness of who and what you are to become common knowledge. It is time for humanity to welcome the Christ within, to bring the kingdom into visibility here on earth.

You are all part of Me. You are all brothers and sisters to each other, yet you see yourselves as separate entities, separate from each other and separate from Me! In the divine reality, you are all one entity, Me, the eternal I Am. Each of you has all knowledge, all wisdom, all understanding. Each of you has/is all you need to instantly bring Me into your world, your reality. You need only know it and want it.

You are not separate from Me. You have merely chosen to appear separate for the purpose of experiencing life as opposed to being life. What you are doing is not so much sin, as you have come to explain pain but unknowing, as is the baby that staggers and falls as it first learns to walk. An infant is totally self-centered. It cries/screams out when its needs are not met.

You unknowing humans cry/scream out when you do not get what you think you need or want, hence you go about fighting and killing each other in your unknowing. When you know, you will no longer choose an unknowing method with which to attain your needs.

Drawing closer to Me, reading that which causes you to truly explore truth as you feel it in your hearts, and coming to know yourselves as neither separate from Me or each other will do a lot to bring humanity past the toddler stage. Many of you are beginning to think outside the box, as you say, but you could also express it as eternal thinking or thinking in the eternal.

Scribe, you have asked several questions. Let us go back and address each one. You asked if you keep coming back until you get it right. Yes and no.

I will endeavor to explain. Think of all the water there is on earth. Some of it is river water; other is pond water. Some is ocean. Other is clean. Some is dirty. Other is salty. And some is fresh. And then there is rain. But it is all water! Regardless of where the water comes from, it all becomes indistinguishable from its source as it returns to the ocean.

You all belong to the Oneness, and each of your individual experiences causes you to grow, to mature, to learn to know who and what you are, and to bring all that information back to the Oneness, ever building on the singular memory of all its learning.

If you are all part of that Oneness, is it any wonder that some of you may actually have recall of parts of the collective memory? Have you, this separate entity you believe to be yourself to be, lived another life or other lives? No, the you that you inhabit as you read this is a unique being. Have you, as part of the great Oneness, lived a life before? Yes, all of them, to greater or lesser degrees!

If you are finding that a particular experiential memory is being presented to your awareness, then know that you are being asked to help work out the pain of this particular unknowing of the collective memory of the Oneness. You are consciously assisting the Oneness to come closer to knowing itself. It is not you, the separate you, who has had to experience lifetimes of pain. You are merely being asked to assist in the growth of the collective consciousness.

You asked, "Do You have some place where we can work out our perfection if our experience of life was not sufficient?"

No! Again I will try to put into words a concept that may be confusing for you to understand depending on how much spiritual exploration you have done to date. When your spirit was created, it was created perfectly so there is no perfection to be worked out! Now you are astounded but also dismissive for most of you are steeped in the concept of an eye for an eye or your understanding of judgment day.

If I told you that life on Earth, as you comprehend it, is merely a dream, an illusion, you would have no difficulty understanding that there is no need for a place for perfecting because you are already perfect. Unfortunately mankind sees itself as separate from Me and separate from each other and will continue to do so until it is known that it is One with Me.

So until you reach that level of consciousness, I have made arrangements to meet you where you are. I entered your world, your illusion, in the form of Jesus Christ, left some insight that was appropriate to the world at that moment in time, and ensured that wisdom would continue to expand by giving you the gift of knowing or what some of you call the Holy Spirit.

The Holy Spirit is My Spirit, available to each and every one of you directly. Each of you is perfectly capable of a direct relationship with Me, and once you know this, you need only desire it and ask.

Perseverance is necessary because that part of you that keeps you believing that this dream or illusion is real, your ego, will work hard to convince you that you are a separate entity who does not behave perfectly and therefore deserves punishment. The Kabbalah refers to it as the bread of shame. Christianity refers to it as original sin.

Because this belief system is so ingrained, I offer My Spirit as solace, mentor, and wisdom to help you all to discover My truth, the knowing that will lead you all to the realization that there is no need for a place of perfecting.

It has taken this scribe quite a few years of spiritual journeying to be able to allow Me to transmit what she just put down on paper, so her concern is that this concept of dream or illusion will be difficult for many of you to accept.

She and I ask you to try something. Think about these concepts that you have just read about over the next few days or weeks, and then see how the ideas resonate within your hearts. If this way of understanding continues to repel you, then that is your choice, and I will continue to be with you wherever you are.

If you find that what we have talked about here elicits a "Yeah, that makes sense" response, then you are ready to grow, to expand your knowing, to think in the eternal. If you are open, I will present you with the bigger picture, so stay present to the moment, and you will find instruction is forthcoming.

You asked, "Do we get punished by our failures to perfect?"

Yes and no. Again I will endeavor to present a response that will provide a satisfactory answer for this moment in time. Yes, you most certainly do get punished by failure to perfect but not by Me and only while you are in human form on earth!

This answer has raised a question in this scribe's mind relating to evil spirits or haunted souls. I will deal with that idea in a moment. Let us first complete the response to punishment. If, as I have said previously, you are already perfect, why would there be any need for punishment? I do not punish!

"Yes, but what about all the bad things people do here on earth?" you ask.

More often than not, the evildoers on earth do reap the rewards of their actions. Though some may appear to have avoided punishment or atonement, the multifaceted aspect of human beings provide many areas in which a human being can suffer, and they are not necessarily visible to others. This is one of the reasons that I ask you not to judge. Leave that up to Me. Judgments merely cause you to reinforce the false belief in separateness.

I repeat. You are all One. When one of you sins, the Oneness notes the sin. When one of you loves, the Oneness notes the love. When the Oneness experiences these things, it extracts the gift of experiential knowledge, so in this way, the Oneness is ever perfecting itself, ever moving toward the collective knowing that you are all One, you are all love, you are all perfect.

Eventually all of you who believe yourselves to be separate from each other will learn to know that you are a collective consciousness that is in the process of perfecting, and once that happens, you will all recognize yourselves as that Oneness and are therefore perfect. Then you will truly understand why there is no need for punishment.

My, how I love you!

0-0

P.S. In regard to evil spirits, you know you have free choice. If that were not so, earth would not exist. Evil spirits, as you call them, are merely spirits that choose to remain separate from the Oneness. There is no need to fear, for fear states that you believe evil to be stronger than I am. You need only pray for them so that part of the Oneness (which is part of you) will eventually come to know truth. And yes, I love them too!

0-0

A DEFINITIVE RESPONSE

*S*cribe, your last thought, "Is there a whispered or implied 'but' at the end of My declaration of unconditional love for each and every one of you?" demands a response.

GG For those in a hurry, the definitive answer is no. There are no conditions to unconditional love! This is one of the most important questions to be asked, so I wish to take time to answer it in a way that leaves no doubt in anyone's mind as to the meaning of this response.

Ever since mankind sensed or became aware of the existence of a power greater than itself, there has been an element of fear associated with that awareness. This was to be expected, for humanity was in its infancy and mere survival was the most important concern. Sometimes fear aids survival.

As you evolved and your know-ledge expanded, you had more time to think. And because humans perceive themselves as separate from Me and each other, your thinking became based in fear. Survival, in the only dimension (incarnation) you knew, became center focus.

As survival became more assured with ever-increasing knowledge, the fear-based humans had time to begin to develop heart knowledge, such things as compassion, insight, awareness of the environment, and love.

With the arrival of these feelings or emotions came the potential to tap into knowing, but because mankind is basically still convinced that each of you is a separate entity and separate from Me, the majority of you still function primarily out of the base emotion of fear.

Slowly you have begun to hear Me. Several centuries of hearing have been recorded and are available to all who are interested, but it is important to remember two things: All hearing is open to interpretation depending on the level of knowing existent within the spiritual seeker, and anyone is capable of hearing regardless of his or her level of knowing. I realize that, for some, this is confusing, but I will endeavour to clarify the statements.

The first statement basically means that, as a person grows spiritually or as mankind increases its collective spiritual knowledge, any statement of truth can have proportionate meaning. For example, a person reading what you refer to as Holy Scripture for the first time will probably take a literal interpretation of what is read. Also if you ask several people who think from the level of their head or ego to read the same passage from Holy Scripture, they will probably have much the same answer. A person with a deep relationship with Me will probably come up with a more multifaceted interpretation. If he or she has begun to explore heart knowing, they may come up with a multitude of varying interpretations. The more you tune in to the vast knowing that resides within yourself, the more you begin to realize that there is seldom a definitive answer to any question. There are some exceptions, like the one that began this communication.

The second statement means I can and will reveal Myself to anyone who is open to being instructed. I am able to transmit wisdom and knowledge to any soul regardless of age, sex, education or lack thereof, position, power, or mental acuity. I can and will use anyone who is willing to be a vessel for the betterment of mankind.

If you are still doubtful but would truly like to understand, not just to pander to your ego but to advance your divine knowing, then sit back comfortably in silence and ask Me to clarify the ideas presented here. As I have said on several occasions, "Anyone is capable of hearing Me, and I speak to anyone who truly desires to know."

0-0

THE EVOLUTION OF SPIRITUALITY

God, Creator of the universe, over the last several months, I have been reading quite a bit: David Hawkins, Eckhart Tolle, Neale Donald Walsh, material on quantum theology, and some of the Christian mystics. God, these people present a vastly different picture to the one the church has presented. Except for a brief breath of fresh air that Pope John XXIII ushered in but lasted only a short while, the teachings of this church remain the same. There seems to be a preoccupation with sin, rarely a mention of God's unconditional love, and a constant reminder that we are not worthy to enter under Your roof. I remember You telling me a long time ago, "I made you worthy when I died on the cross for you!" Except for Sunday mass shared with a priest I respect and a community that helps me feel that I belong, I have little interest anymore in what goes on at the Vatican. The Catholic faith that is dispensed from Rome at this time saddens me.

NB This material was completed before the arrival of Pope Francis. As I now am preparing this manuscript for publication (2017), I have much hope of another breath of fresh air in the Vatican.

The material I have been reading in all these books resonates within, which is convincing me that it is closer to Your truth. My

God, You seem to be also suggesting that the gift of healing, both for myself and others, is to be explored and mastered. Papa, my body is giving me quite a bit of reason to listen to this directive, for pain and fear of pain are slowing me down and draining my previous enthusiasm.

Having sent off the third manuscript and having heard nothing, I'm feeling pretty much like a waste of space, and I know this is just my perception, but I think I could use Your input right about now.

☙

Annava, My Annava,

My precious friend, do not cry! When have you ever seen the downside of your life not become the ashes out of which you rise? You see yourself as a slow learner, someone who wastes much time playing Spider and Solitaire on the computer when you could be cleaning, ironing, exercising, writing, going for a walk, and so forth. You fault yourself and find yourself wanting when it comes to doing for others or giving to charity. You see yourself as a failure, for no one you have prayed for has ever been instantly healed and your own pain has been grinding your nerves raw.

Today you feel quite empty, not so much depressed as just empty, as though you are perfectly satisfied with just being, waiting for the next person who needs you. This morning you just appreciated a goldfinch sitting on the edge of the birdbath in close proximity to you as you watered the garden.

Ann, do you not see the change that is slowly taking place within you? You are beginning to become familiar with whom you really are (whom you have always been) that which has been buried under all the perceptions of who and what you have believed others have wanted you to be. You are beginning to think for yourself and listen to the voice/spirit/Oneness within that conveys truth to those who listen.

GG Life is about relationship, the relationship of people with their God, each other, and self, not with institutions run by leaders who perceive themselves to be having all the answers.

For quite some time, I have been making sure that you are learning to see the bigger picture. The world is ready to move beyond its self-centered mentality, and to do that, wisdom, knowing, and truth must begin to be 'within' people. You have picked up the expression, "collective consciousness," which is the fastest way to spread the good news.

Part of this good news is that life is what you make it. At this moment in time, you see that playing itself out as the unenlightened powers-that-be play at trying to be the best at whatever they do for themselves. The preoccupation with what is good for me or us needs to change to what is the best for all of us, and you happen to be someone who is ready to hear a better version of who you are meant to be.

Why you? For that matter, why anyone who finds himself or herself in exactly the same or similar circumstances? As I said to you years ago, Annie, why not you?

As a moderate number of people busy themselves with war, patriotism, religious fundamentalism, and base self-centeredness and greed, there is quite a growth of belief developing in others that the old way, the separate way, is no longer a valid approach to life here on earth. As more and more people become disheartened by what is being offered by the leaders and manufacturers of goods and services, they begin to turn inward, and there eventually they will find ultimate truth, wisdom, and compassion. When enough people have discovered this truth within themselves, the old way will just break down, and new leaders with vision will emerge from the masses. Mankind will take the next quantum leap forward toward becoming an ever-perfecting expression of Oneness. How do you like them apples, Annie?

☙

That feels right, Lord. May I ask one more question?

☙

Of course!

☙

What about the pain? Am I to accept, expecting my spine to continue to deteriorate as it is said that it will, or is there something that You are expecting me to learn and pass on? My biggest concern is that I will fail to have the required amount of faith to overcome my doubts in my ability to get it right!

I know that miracles do occur. You worked one with my anxiety all those years ago, but then I knew nothing. I just screamed out to You in utter frustration. Now I know that faith in You works miracles. How do I expand my faith so I can get to the point where I just know that You work through me to heal others and myself?

☙

Annava, you really do want to learn this stuff, don't you?

☙

Yes, Lord, I do! I'd love to be able to silently walk through life fixing things. When I see people in difficult situations, pain, disfigurement, fear, loneliness, and disease, I'd give anything to be able to say just a few words of encouragement to them, knowing that soon Your miracle would become evident to them and their faith in You would grow. I don't want to become famous. I just want to do what you see that I could do, quietly and without fanfare and hoopla. Maybe I could even have left the scene before the miracle occurs.

☙

Ann, hear Me. I do want to use you. I do want to give you this gift, but I want others to come to know that it is a gift available to all. As this world is changing, don't you think that this would be an ideal tool for the betterment of all?

What I want you to do now is document these next few months with Me. Yes, right here in this manuscript. Whenever you sense My call, come and write about your pain and the pain of those I send your way. If you want people to come to know, trust, and love Me, they are going to have to get to know that I am trustworthy and all loving.

Enough for today. Go and have a moderate lunch, and then get on with the bills that you so often doubt that My skillful resources can meet.

Love,

0-0

A HEALING UPDATE

You have asked me to respond to the call to write. Lord, a few things have happened. After I wrote down our last communication, a friend came over that evening, and she read it. She has done something to her leg, which is making it very difficult to be up and down ladders, thinning peaches, and picking cherries.

We commented that this ability to heal ourselves and each other seems to be the thrust of Your instruction lately, and we decided to pray together for the healing of her leg. ("Whenever two or more are gathered in My name.") I can no longer remember all that was said, but as we put our hands together, I asked if she sensed that we should put our hands on her knee.

She paused for a moment and then said, "They're okay where they are."

"Is there somewhere else we should place our hands?" I queried.

A brief moment later, she responded, "It's not my knee. It's my heart that needs to heal."

I remember asking that my doubt in myself would not get in the way of anything You had to do for her, and eventually she headed home.

She called yesterday morning to say that something had happened last night and she was now running up and down stairs, pain-free. There was some comment about not knowing how it would be at the end of a busy day in the orchard, but for now, she was pain-free.

Second, I have been praying for another friend, a lady in her mid-eighties who has suffered from arthritis since the day after the arrival of her first child in her early twenties. Recently her left shoulder has frozen, and that has been where I have been focusing my prayers. I told her a week or so ago that I was doing this and asked her to stay open to You.

Yesterday we had the opportunity to actually pray together. She told me about going in to church on Sunday, and as she sat down, she felt a hand on her left shoulder. She turned to respond to whomever was there, but no one was there. She continued to feel a gentle pressure on that shoulder, which caused her to turn a second time, just to make sure. Again, there was no one.

She had since taken a bit of a tumble and hurt her shoulder again, so yesterday when we prayed together, we focused on the shoulder, the overall arthritis, and any other deep, long-seated hurt that may need to be resolved. Again I asked that I might step out of the way and let You do what needed to be done.

That is all that seems to be relevant up to this moment. Lord, what is Your input, or did you just need me to record the experiences?

CR

Annie,

GG Thank you for stepping out of your comfort zone and offering something that you do not believe you possess. I realize that your major concern is that, if you pray for someone and they hear you asking for something and it is not forthcoming, they will lose faith and trust in Me. You do not wish to be the cause of someone else drawing away from Me due to disappointment.

Annie, I have good and bad news. The good news is that they probably will not draw away from Me, but they will probably doubt **your** healing abilities.

⚛

But I don't heal anyway, Lord. You do!

⚛

That is not altogether accurate, Annie. We do it together! You are quite right. Alone, you cannot heal yourself or others, and I don't need to use one of you humans to heal another, but when one of you aligns themselves with Me for the betterment of the world, we have liftoff!

In your case, I healed you directly for you hardly knew Me, and there were none around you with any greater knowledge. I had to heal you directly. That healing convinced you beyond a shadow of a doubt that I existed.

This work of salvation will happen more quickly if I can use more of you to work with Me in this plan. I am calling many directly to do this work, and I have chosen you as one of them because we can tell even more souls to be open to My promptings through your writings. Yes, I hear your silent thoughts. "How can my writings get anyone interested if I can't even get the books published?" All in good time, Annie!

Now regarding your friends and all other people who present their pain to you, you never need worry about timing or whether I would heal them or not. Healing is a given. Timing is when they are ready. What has to be healed is the next point of focus. Sometimes it may be obvious like a bleeding wound, but more often, discernment is called for.

In the case of your first friend, she wound up telling you what needed healing, her heart. In the case of the older friend, you prayed for her acknowledged pain, but your words probed more deeply into the past for possible causative factors. You are correct in allowing My healing to go where it divinely knows to go. The only correction that I wish to impart is that, from now on, do not dismiss yourself from the healing moment. You are the conduit through which My healing power flows.

The idea here is to help people to realize that this is a gift that is their heritage as sons and daughters of an all-powerful, compassionate, forgiving King. This is My gift to you for your use. You are not separate from it. It is part of you, just as your arms, legs, hair, and eyes are part of you.

The effectiveness of the gift will strengthen as you continue to practice on yourself and others. You are well aware of your egoic side, Annie. Do not be afraid of it getting in the way. I know your heart, and I entrust some of this work to you. Come now, and We will work a little longer together in Oneness.

0-0

ANOTHER HEALING UPDATE

Our friend Linda, who has more often than not been in a state of angst and for whom I have been praying for quite a while, was over last evening. She told me she had something she wished to share with me.

On a particular day this week, she experienced rightness for the first time in her life. Rightness may best be defined as being at peace with who she is, where she lives, and the circumstances in which she finds herself in this moment in time. She said it lasted all day and she had no desire to run. Most of the time she's running, running from her home or what she senses her home represents. She attributes this brief awareness, knowing, or peace to prayers that her counsellor said in tongues, and she added she knew I was praying for her. Any comment, Lord?

◊

Annie,

GG *You are beginning to get a bit of feedback that tells you that prayer works, not just a hurried request that a particular problem might disappear, but the surrounding of the person in My divine embrace and a request to heal the inner person. Keep practicing. Don't give up on yourself either. Your own healing is important to this whole experience.*

Your failure yesterday to clear up your left ankle (considerable vein discoloration, swelling, and skin blemishes) says nothing other than you are learning that this healing is not magic but a natural process that is effective when you understand the process. Hangeth thou in there!

0-0

LEARNING HOW TO APPRECIATE OURSELVES

God, this does not seem to have anything to do with healing, but I already have two manuscripts going, and You seem to be urging me to write about this here. Our cat is causing me considerable irritation. Whenever I sit down, she's there wanting to be scratched. She can be anywhere in the house, but the moment I sit for any reason, she appears and either stands on her hind legs and taps my arm with one of her forepaws or just jumps up beside me if possible.

There is a resentful reaction that I notice within myself, and I'm wondering if You are using this creature to make me aware of something. She seems to have a need for constant attention. Why is this irritating me? She's only a cat?

֍

GG Well, Annie, I thought you would never get the message! I'm delighted to respond, and it fits in here just perfectly. I know you cannot see how, and you are concerned that this will reveal some embarrassing characteristic within yourself, right? When have I ever embarrassed you in our communications?

When someone grows up in a family where their thoughts, interests, and dreams go unnoticed, they have a tendency to believe that their thoughts, wishes, and dreams do not matter. If nothing happens to change that philosophy as they get older, they withdraw into themselves. There is a continuous search for identity which tells them in a worldly sense who and what they are. If nothing and no one activates the development process, they are forever looking to others for affirmation of themselves.

Even though I stepped into your life several years ago and took you under My wing, so to speak, your original upbringing is still part of who you are, and I did not choose to zap you into awareness. I wanted you to acquire it naturally from experience.

Yes, Ann, it had to take this long! You are beginning to get a very real sense of who you really are, and the irritation you feel toward the cat is merely being allowed to show you that you are an integral part of other peoples' lives even when you are not interacting with them at the moment. What is the correlation in all these things? I will explain.

Your cat came into your household as a very young stray. Obviously she got separated from her litter experience before she realized that cats are independent, totally satisfied to just be a cat with no need for humans other than easy food and a warm place to sleep. Your cat is still trying to discover this truth.

May I suggest that you set up a petting and grooming routine in the day, and once you have acknowledged her once or twice a day, you will find she becomes much less demanding. If only humans were so easily convinced!

Now why are you reacting to this constant demand for attention? You've learned to live without attention, or have you? Aren't you still comparing yourself to others? When are you going to accept, respect, and cherish who you are? All the acclaim in the world will have no impact at all if you do not treasure who you are. And that is what healing is about!

ANN MONSTER

Don't you think that this is a perfect focus for the end of this communication, helping others to see themselves through God glasses or as I see them! What an incredible place this world will become when everyone knows himself or herself as a precious heir of God!

Love,

Pops AKA 0-0

MORE HEALING DOCUMENTATIONS

On Sunday after church, a brief comment led me to ask someone if they would like prayers to surround an investigative procedure that they were having done this morning at this very moment. We prayed, she had tears in her eyes, and we went our separate ways. I prayed I would remember to be alert at eleven thirty on Tuesday morning, the time of the procedure.

At about eleven twenty-five, I sat down to play the piano, and the sheet music in front of me was "Here I Am, Lord." As I started to play, I instantly remembered my friend, and this was her moment. I went and sat quietly. I envisioned Jesus and I both standing in the procedure room, first aware of the fear she might still be experiencing. And after dealing with that, our focus became her lungs and then the skill of the doctor and attendants.

I was wondering if Teresa's* spirit was free to join with Jesus and me, and the next moment, my mind was off thinking of my husband Bert, who had gone off for a bicycle ride without his helmet. Fear entered.

At that moment, I sensed Jesus gently asking me to leave the room, for my fear was not appropriate. I actually felt embarrassed. I left, sat out on the steps for a moment or two until I could refocus, and then went back, knowing I was welcome as soon as I was ready. After a short while, I returned to my day. No major miracles yet, Lord.

I was talking to Nadia this morning. She's the one with the leg that was so painful while climbing up and down ladders, picking fruit. When I asked her how her leg was, she said the excruciating pain was gone, but it was tired and sore by the end of a working day. I suggested she keep open to Your voice in case there was still something to which You wished her to be alert. Any comments, Lord?

૭

We're doing just fine. Keep at it, and be patient. You handled the rejection of your manuscript yesterday very well. You did not allow disappointment to stop you from hearing Me so you know where to send it next.

0-0

*Teresa was a highschool friend, one of my bridesmaids and died in her fifties.

૭

I have another update. The lady whose lungs were being scoped reported an extremely easy procedure. She was astounded at how peaceful she was throughout the process and that there was no sore throat afterward.

Yesterday after mass, she was waiting for me. A couple weeks have passed since the test, and by now she had results.

I asked her, "So what are we dealing with?"

She smiled, saying, "There is no cancer, no bronchitis, and no tuberculosis." She had envisioned them all.

What they did discover were a couple of microorganisms that she had been aware of for some years and another one that was new to her. The doctor's concern was the limitations her allergies put on the antibiotics that he would be able to prescribe.

So yesterday we again prayed, asking God to do whatever needed to be done to bring this lady's lungs to wholeness. Further tests would be carried out in a month or two after the present medications have had time to do their job. Thank You, God, for getting her this far.

○○

You're welcome, Annie. Now tell them about Nadia.

○○

At a luncheon last week, Nadia's opening remarks as we sat down were, "Oh, by the way, I did what you had said and asked God why the pain returned only at night."

I had suggested to her that maybe You still had some insights that You wished to impart. The pain was merely one way to keep her focused long enough at the end of a tiring day to hear what You needed to say. She did not give details, but she was quite surprised and pleased with the instruction she received.

Thank You again, Lord!

○○

You are welcome again, Annie. No, don't put your pen down yet.

My precious Annie,

GG We've talked about healing. We've talked about other people's healing. Now it is time to deal with the tying up of loose ends that still have the ability to limit your potential.

You spend much of your time dealing with others. You rarely see the friends with whom you just have fun. Those you do see or hear from the most are those who need you, and as a result, you feel drained pretty much most of the time.

॰॰॰

Lord Jesus, am I making this up so as to justify the multiple days that pass that seem to have no purpose or accomplishment component? I can sit for hours doing crosswords or jigsaw puzzles but seldom feel that I have accomplished anything.

॰॰॰

Annie, I hear you. I know you. I understand what makes you tick even if you do not. You function out of your core being. I use this expression because heart and soul have taken on new meaning with all the reading you have been doing, and I want you to be utterly clear with the meaning of My words.

At this moment in time, your core being is trying to assimilate your awareness of Me with who and what you perceive yourself to be. Between the two of Us, We are trying to help you to move beyond your physical self and align yourself more frequently with your spiritual self. Though you say that you accomplish very little, you are more often than not speaking to Me on one level or another.

I know you are having a hard time believing this, but I assure you that you are frequently in communion with Me, and I ask no more of you for now. Your time to attend to activities that can be evaluated will come. For now, you are in the final stages of preparation, practice, and personal healing.

Keep your readers apprised of your own progress as well as the feedback you receive from others.

☙

Well then, Lord, I should conclude with Your instructive just a couple hours ago. I was berating myself for my continuing inability to lose weight. Your comment to me went something like, *"Annie, you have to be willing, and I will do the rest!"* I hear You, Jesus. Thank You. I will try to do my best.

THE POWER OF POSITIVE THINKING

*A*nother step has been presented in my staircase of learning and awareness. Lord, do You want me to elaborate, or would it be clearer to the reader if You do?

ᛤ

Annie, I would like you to begin.

ᛤ

Two weeks ago, our friend Linda came over with a DVD that a friend of hers had suggested she watch. It was called *The Secret*, a documentary on the power of attraction. The power of positive thinking was a concept we heard about years ago, and now this DVD and other writers are scientifically reinforcing the concept on a regular basis. When I first watched this video, I had tears running down my face. Something within me was reacting to what was being presented. I have been drawn to watch this material over and over again, and each time I watch it, I seem to get more out of it. Something is being reinforced.

Just prior to this information being introduced to me, I was close to a panic state regarding a leak in our roof, which was dripping into the house over the front door. The shingles were not old enough to be the cause of leaking, but regardless, we could not afford to have the roof re shingled. Would the manufacturer honor the twenty-five year guarantee? When I spoke to the fellow over the phone, he did not sound even remotely interested or helpful! Our car was also overheating. How would we come up with this amount of money to resolve these issues? I was experiencing a very negative, panicky mood, which was quite out of character with the usual serenity that has been a seemingly constant in my life for several years.

ଔ

Annie, may I continue?

ଔ

Please do!

ଔ

Thank you for explaining to our readers the beginning of what you have had presented to you.

GG I remind them that I did not cause the roof to leak or the car to overheat. I merely allowed these natural occurrences to become useful teaching tools.

ଔ

I needed you to have a definite understanding of how negatively you were approaching life—do not have enough money, cannot find an interested publisher for my next book, cannot lose this weight, and having physical issues and associated pain.

I needed you to be alert so the concepts in the DVD that would be coming your way would leap out at you. I needed to prepare you to be open to the *concepts presented in MAP, the other information I had presented to you in these last few weeks.*

Annie, you have been asking to know more about what is offered to the human race. What is the potential of each individual in relation to the bigger picture? How can you help yourself and others to find healing and abundance when the world seems to be doing a nosedive?

You are realizing that We are coming to the end of this copybook. Let Us use the remaining pages to document some physical manifestations of what mankind has the potential to expect from life on earth.

To date, it has been difficult, for a vast majority of you and that was not—nor is—our original intent. You have had many visionaries over the centuries, but to date, few have had the insight as to how to propel people and these powerful concepts into the mainstream of human imagining.

We are going to try to do that here. We are going to intend to convince individuals (because it is within the individual hearts that these concepts must take root) that life in abundance is expected to be the norm and can be achieved by some paradigm shifting in a few areas of human perception.

We are going to help individuals to understand their human potential as seen through the eyes of God.

O-O

THE IMPORTANCE OF TRULY KNOWING OURSELVES

*D*ear God, I want to explain the insight I received today, but I'm wondering if it would be better if You were the one putting it into words.

༒

Give it a try yourself. It will manifest more quickly if it becomes an understandable and comfortable concept for you.

༒

I did what is called a "map calibration process" this morning. In that process, I asked why I have repeatedly maintained being overweight all my life when I truly believe that I want to be thinner and feel healthier. I can lose a bit. I can be addiction-free for short periods of time, but inevitably I give in and cease trying. The answer I received seemed to be as follows: As an infant, I was not wanted. I was not loved. I was not held. I was put down as soon as possible. I was emotionally abandoned.

When my awareness responded with, "I already knew this," I was informed that, yes, as an adult, I had come to know this, to understand how my mother could have been feeling and to forgive her totally. What had not yet happened was for that abandoned infant psyche to heal—to come to know that its pain has been acknowledged—and to know I have now held it and loved it in my own arms. Then another thought arose. Do I have to forgive her/me for being the reason for my perpetual failure to love myself enough to look after me? Well, God, am I inspired here or just rambling?

☙

Annie, My precious one, you are on the home stretch!

☙

God, I finished last night's writing with, "You are on the home stretch." This morning, in spite of feeling yesterday that I need not pursue another map process before next week, I sensed I should do one right then and there. This time, Your Son was extremely present, and it was as though I could feel my love for Him growing from moment to moment. I was reminded of the power that He could manifest. Was I being given some of that same power, God, for it felt as though something strong had been fixed in my chest?

A sharp pain in my left leg just below the knee was periodically distracting me, and eventually I placed my hand over the ache. It took much encouragement from You for me to imagine my new energy. Eventually I felt some warmth on my leg. I must have drifted into sleep, for as I attempted to come to, the pain was gone. I wanted to stay where I was, but I thought I heard a voice call my name to wake me up. (I was alone in the house.) So I forced myself to waken.

I went to get the mail thinking to myself, "I must imagine checks in the mail if the law of attraction has any credibility". Immediately

I curbed my thoughts, knowing how quickly and easily I could get disappointed.

There was an (unexpected) check in the mail for Bert for his presentation on Henri Nouwen. I laughed. There was another check for Bert the following day from a newspaper that has never before paid him for his submitted articles. The priest at church on Sunday handed him a check to cover his teaching expenses, and I actually received an order for a few of my books.

Yesterday, I experienced an intense sense of this power that You seem to be implying is mine. I felt overwhelmed, and the tears started to roll. Then the thought came that maybe I was probably making it all up in my mind. Am I spending an inordinate amount of time thinking about all this, and am I losing my grip on reality?

Quite early this morning, a severe thunderstorm was coming our way, and I stood at the window watching the energy bouncing around the sky before the rain and thunder began to accompany the lightning. Again what You had said yesterday about giving me power came to mind. I realized that something had changed within me. For the first time in months, I feel energized. I feel a sense of worth. It's as though part of me has been away and has finally come home. I feel different, but it is so subtle that I really don't know how else to express it. Lord, do I need to say more, or do You wish to comment?

☙

Annie, put the pen down now. We'll talk later.

☙

Our friend Linda has done something to her back. When she came over Friday evening, she asked if I would try some healing. As You know, I did pray quietly for a couple minutes. She called the next evening to tell me that the pain was gone. In fact, she could not remember even having it after the prayers. Thank You!

ଔ

Thank you, Annie.

O-O

ALL IN GOD'S TIMING

*L*ord, I am struggling. The problem of the roof repair is taking some detours as we try to get it resolved. The amount of rain we've been having is not helping either. I do not know why it is distressing me so much, but it is.

Today is our thirty-eighth wedding anniversary, and half a jug of rainwater was inside the front door this morning. We got the estimate or offer from one roofer, but when we contacted the previous roofer to put their offer in dollars and cents, we were informed that they would not be able to do our roof until next year. We put in a call to someone else for advice, but they have not called back yet.

The car's indicator lights were clicking too fast or not working at all, but when we drove over to the garage, they ceased malfunctioning. Our new electric kettle that we purchased last week went on the fritz today, so we had to take it back. The salesgirl was actually very helpful!

My positive thinking (not very positive today) did not cause my lottery ticket to produce even a free ticket, and I'm just a tad (actually a lot) discouraged with my negativity.

Lord, I know I am supposed to think positive thoughts, to act as if money is not a problem (the roof or the car). I know I am to be grateful, and I am trying to be, but I am not impressed with my success rate. I do not want to fail at producing positive results in this life of mine just because somewhere way back I came to believe "nice things do not happen to Ann Richardson" (Monster).

How do I change? How do I get to that point of expecting and just knowing that what I want will happen when most of my living experience has taught me otherwise?

ଓଃ

GG Annie, I hear you. I see your concern, and I know how hard you are trying. I know you are attempting to steer clear of feeling sorry for yourself, but do not defeat yourself because everything does not come easily or without a struggle. Your roof will get done this year. Yes, you are hearing Me. You are not making it up. You already know how to pay for it if the actual bill is more than your cash on hand.

As far as your ability to be positive, causing positive things to happen around you, we are working on this aspect of your growth together. Just keep at it and keep working on the healing of yourself and others. If you see some progress, it will encourage you to know that this is truly something I am presenting to you to use should you sense a need for our involvement.

No, Annie, becoming aware of energy is not moving away from Me. I am energy! I am merely teaching you more about Myself, and seeing as how I live in you, then what I am is yours.

Do not give up. You do have the ability to learn these ways and to use them with wisdom. I neither waste My time nor yours. Persist and trust!

0-0

ଓଃ

The roof was done last week. It is so nice to no longer be distressed each time it rains, and it has been doing a lot of that this fall. Lord, I continue to strive to be positive. I did pay for the roof with a line of credit check, for we had only half the amount necessary in savings. The company did a good job, and the workers were great. The problems with the car seemed to eventually get resolved, and I continue to try to stay positive. My spine is giving me reminders that it is degenerating, and I am trying to convince it that it has the option not to, but with each new twinge, I fear I am losing the upper hand.

I was supposed to work with our daughter today, removing paper for a customer of hers. The thought of bending over and scrubbing down walls was not appealing to me. So Bert, bless his heart, agreed to go in my place. Friday, I'm supposed to be hanging the new paper.

Lord, what is going to happen to me? Are the years I have left destined to be painful and immobile? Pain pulls out the carpet from under my most positive intentions. I do not want to fill these pages with my miseries. That is not uplifting to any reader. Do I need to add anything else, or are You willing to take it from here? I am listening.

Okay, I hear You. You remind me that my emotions are telling me that I am out of alignment with what I truly want. Change focus, right?

గ్ర

Right! Well done! You're learning. What you really want is to be pain-free, and that requires time for those sensitive areas of your back to heal. Do not sit worrying about tomorrow, Friday, next week, or even next year. Stay focused on the little bit of healing that must occur today. Eventually all those little bits will begin to feel like a whole lot. Take something for the pain if you feel that might help, and stop focusing on what you are unable to do. Concentrate on what you can do and be grateful for all you do accomplish. This too will pass. You are never alone.

0-0

DOING IT JESUS' WAY

Dear God, an ever-strengthening movement called fundamentalism seems to be putting down roots everywhere. Even this broad term covers several areas of selectivism, that is, "Yes, I believe in Christ but …." Catholicism seems to be trying to go back to basics. The fundamentalist Muslims are busy justifying their beliefs with killings, bombings, and other terrorist attacks. The Jewish people are merely defending themselves by insisting on having what was always theirs. Everyone is hurting, and we all look to the others, pointing fingers of blame to explain our unease.

Lord, we are all looking for answers, but instead of asking You for insight, we turn to power seekers who offer overly simplified back-to-basics type of answers that hint at the justification of separating oneself from those who do not think exactly as oneself.

We need Your wisdom, God. We need to put on God glasses to see clearly our future and the direction that we should be taking. Lord, You have given us all free choice, and I have come to believe that You offer us all resurrection regardless of the road or path onto which we were born or later choose.

How do we move toward a loving relationship with You, all our neighbors, and particularly ourselves? Please shed some light that all human beings can embrace, right where they are. What do we need to do to truly live fulfilling, joy-filled lives that reflect You and all You know we can achieve? Your input, please, and give me the grace to hear a truth to which every one of Your offspring can hear and relate.

☙

My precious scribe, it is good to be working with you again in this manuscript. Your own personal issues, healing, and growth have challenged your energies. You continue to make progress.

GG Mankind is beginning to wake up (to think) and to move beyond what has always been believed into what truly is.

As knowledge (provable fact) expands, it seems to some folks that the bigger picture and safe faith are not compatible, and to a certain degree, they are not. Safe faith states that there is a black-and-white formula, which, if followed to the letter, will safely bring you to the pearly gates of God's heavenly realm. It takes all the guesswork out of that spiritual aspect of life giving you more time and energy to concentrate on coping with the evil in this world.

The bigger picture approach is exciting for those who are ready to embrace it, but it causes fear for the person who still does not realize just how awesome each one of you is just because you are all My creation, My offspring, a part of Me.

When you believe you are separate from Me, you choose mediocrity over excellence. When you choose mediocrity, you see yourselves as basically bad, evil, sin-oriented souls, still needing to do something to redeem yourselves.

Jesus came to earth for the express purpose of revealing the truth. He stated your mission as three directives. He asked you to love the Father (through

Him if that would make the task clearer), love your neighbor (which means everyone with no exceptions), and love yourself (as I will make every effort to treat myself respectfully, lovingly, and compassionately as I work toward ever perfecting). That is what He said in a nutshell.

If you follow those guidelines, it does not justify killing, hating, or ignoring anyone who does not think exactly as you do. If you are following these guidelines, you don't say, "Yes, Jesus died for our sins but …" There are no buts!

Do you truly think that your salvation depends on something you have to do? Would that not make what Christ did for you impotent? Your free choices, good or bad, affect your life and the lives of others here on earth. They do not derail God's will. Nothing is greater or more powerful than God so how could anything overpower God's plan!?

0-0

CHAOS—WHERE DO WE BEGIN?

Dear God, there has been another multiple killing in a school in the States. Someone takes a gun and shoots as many people as possible. Why? For what purpose? What causes such an act, Lord? How can we correct the damage done to a person that would cause him or her to do such a futile thing? How do we re-educate ourselves in the areas that are obviously being ignored in our societies? How do we stop pointing fingers at others as the cause of the problem and start to work together for solutions? Lord God, we desperately need Your wisdom!

☙

To all who are hurting, this is where you must begin.

GG Hurt is at the root of all the ills that mankind experiences. You believe yourselves to be at the mercy of anything that comes along because you see yourselves as separate, separate from each other and most certainly from Me.

So many of you are convinced that the simple directive you were given—to love Me, your neighbor, and yourselves—has no significance in this present age. Yet I reassure you that it is still the fastest method of correction available to the human race.

God Glasses

Think of a room in which a handful of like-minded people are meeting to discuss something in which they all share an interest. So far so good. During the course of their dialoguing, someone suggests something to which another disagrees, and that is still okay because that is why these people have come together, to iron out a problem, to find solutions, and to decide a course of action.

The problem arises when opposition to the suggested solution is presented in a derogatory manner, which offends one or more people. Feelings are hurt, people take sides, and the mood in the room changes all because someone chose to speak in a manner that he himself would not appreciated if it had been directed toward him. Love your neighbour as yourself.

The outcome of the meeting will depend on what sort of a person the chair or moderator is. If this person is a caring and committed moderator, the results will probably be positive. If you have a moderator who has to be right, is afraid of confrontation, is a people pleaser, or has any number of less than honest characteristics, the outcome is open to a variety of results, all with the potential to be negative.

Unfortunately it does not end when the meeting is over. If someone's pride has been hurt, it will rankle. Some will side with the perpetrator; others will side with the victim. And so begins any confrontation.

When one person's needs are not met on a continuing basis, that individual will attempt to ease his own pain one way or another. If his life experience has been perceived as one of ongoing deprivation, pain, or suffering, he might very well get to the point of utter frustration and react in an inappropriate way.

This is an oversimplified explanation of what goes on in the world on a daily basis. When a strong-willed soul gets frustrated enough, it erupts and often hurts those in close proximity. When a gentle soul gets frustrated enough, it quite often opts out of living either by withdrawal or death.

To keep it in simplest terms, everyone must learn a kinder way to behave.

0-0

LIVING WITHIN TIME

*D*ear God, a statement that is becoming more familiar in present-day writings is "time is an illusion." Time is something that we humans experience because of our choice to see ourselves separate from each other and, in particular, from You.

Lord, this morning as I was walking by the lake, You seemed to impress on my thoughts, "I am always constant and the same. I do not change." It gave me a great deal of peace as I absorbed the concept, but I do not know exactly why. I sense You have asked me to write today in this manuscript, so if I have perceived correctly, this pen is Yours.

☙

Annie, My precious Annie and all My precious friends,

GG Time has such an influence on your lives. Many of you express such sentiments as, "Where does the time go? I'm running out of time. There's never enough time." Others complain of having too much time on their hands, or the days (or nights) are so long.

When I impressed upon your minds that "I am constant and unchanging," I was attempting to give you all another piece of the puzzle. To fully utilize all you are through Me, you have to understand what I am, and one of the divine characteristics is constancy, that which does not change. Everything in your world, especially that which you hold most dear, is constantly changing—your thoughts, feelings, likes, dislikes, finances, health, relationships, age, and so on.

You are submerged in inconstancy and change. Is it any wonder that you have a tendency to be drowning in fear? You see yourselves as being at the mercy of an unfriendly world, and in essence, as long as you perceive yourselves as separate from each other and Me, you are at the mercy of an unfriendly world. Some places and people are more unfriendly than others are.

*What I want to say to you is this. If all of you could collectively stop being afraid, your world would instantaneously change for the better. Barring Me butting in where I have not been invited, this is not likely to occur very quickly. There **is** something you can each do on an individual basis that can certainly get you started in the right direction.*

First, I am going to give you an analogy that should help to put all this into perspective. Think of yourself as driving along a beautiful country road. You come to a fork in the road and have to decide which way to go. After you have driven down one of these roads a short distance, you realize it is heading you into a very busy expressway.

Driving here is much different from the beautiful laneway. Now you have to concentrate, watching in all directions for split-second decisions that might have to be made. Eventually you get to exit this breakneck pace, and once again, peace, serenity, and beauty surround you. Here comes the analogy.

The country lane represents eternal life. The auto route represents life as you experience it here on earth. You have always been and will always be with Me and part of Me. For a brief moment in time, you slip into time and exist as a human being. And then you slip back out of time into the

Oneness of constancy, that which never changes. I am that which never changes. I am love. Therefore you are love! Now you have a little better understanding of who you are in relation to Me.

Second, we'll address how best to express that brief moment in time. Believe it or not, you do not take the trip into time unwillingly or unknowingly. Regardless of how your time plays out, you have chosen the experience willingly, knowing beforehand exactly how it will turn out. Each moment in time has purpose that will either slow or quicken the pace of the eternal plan. I make Myself available to all and anyone who chooses to utilize all I offer.

The more you wish to understand your part and how you can positively affect the day-to-day outcomes in your world, the more power-filled you will become. I will instruct you personally. Just leave yourself open to a sense of knowing.

The more of you who choose to make a difference, the sooner My plan for mankind reaches fruition. Any one life will be vastly improved if it has Me at the helm, and all you have to do to ensure My guidance is to invite Me to transmit it to you.

0-0

BON VOYAGE!

*D*earest God, once again, another copybook has been filled up. This one has been a work in progress for six years. You have asked me to close this set of communications. As I reread the previous entry, I wonder if it is a teaser, luring the reader on to great promises. And then the book ends! I feel we need Your input here, Lord.

☙

Thank you, Annie.

GG You are quite correct. After reading this book, the reader will have gained a better understanding of mankind's intended relationship with Me, the Godhead. Time to absorb this new understanding is necessary before one is ready and able to even begin to absorb that to which I was referring in the previous communication.

I also wanted to plant the seed of interest in our readers' hearts so they have more to think about and search out after they put this book back on a shelf. I want them to begin to ponder what the Scripture quote, "This and more you shall do," might actually mean. My desire is to give mankind the opportunity to fully understand all that is being offered to you as children of the one all-powerful, all-knowing, and all-loving God.

I have asked you to inscribe My words in a manner that is easy to understand and utilize so anyone who might be interested in a relationship with Me has access to some useful pointers.

We will close now with just a few words of encouragement. Know that I read hearts even if prayer and relationship with Me are not yet a part of your daily activities. I can lead you where you want to go, and you can speed up the process if you include Me in your travel plans.

Know that My timing is seldom the same as yours, as I do not live within time. I am not affected by time. Time only affects your physical world. Therefore, be patient with Me, as I have and will always be patient with you.

Regardless of who you are or what you have done, are doing, and have yet to do, I have the ability to see your divine potential. So never give up on yourself or Me, cease believing that I punish, and remember that My name is Love.

Answers will be forthcoming when you listen to My voice within you. Always use your God glasses.

Love,

God